Wealth
Unlocked

Your Path to Financial Freedom

By
Np Chambers

Wealth Unlocked

Your Path to Financial Freedom

Table of Contents

Introduction

Welcome to a journey where financial independence isn't a distant dream but a reachable reality. Many people spend their entire lives in pursuit of wealth, not realizing that true financial freedom isn't about the dollar amount in your bank account. Instead, it's about making your money work for you, paving the way for a life without the constraints of financial pressure. This book is here to guide you on this enlightening path, using strategies that are practical, relatable, and achievable.

The path to financial independence is one that demands understanding, discipline, and a little courage. It starts with redefining what wealth means to you personally. Once you embrace the idea that wealth isn't just about accumulation but about creating opportunities and choices, you begin to see the possibilities unfold before you. You don't need to have a rich uncle or a lottery ticket; what you need is knowledge and the willingness to take action. And that's what this book aims to deliver—a comprehensive guide packed with time-tested principles and innovative strategies.

In this transformative journey, you'll find that mastering personal finance is akin to mastering your habits. The discipline of managing your expenses, understanding debt, and prioritizing savings will build a strong foundation upon which you can construct your financial empire. Each chapter in this book meticulously lays down elements of wealth-building like pieces of a well-crafted puzzle. You'll not only learn how to budget effectively or manage debt but also how to utilize the tools and resources that turn savings into wealth-generating investments.

Understanding investments can be intimidating, yet this book simplifies those complexities. Whether you're learning the basics of stocks and bonds, exploring the intricacies of real estate, or diving into business ventures, this guide breaks down concepts into digestible pieces. Each chapter not only educates but also motivates, encouraging you to think big while educating you on how to execute with precision.

But beyond strategies and techniques, this journey towards financial independence requires a shift in mindset. Adopting a wealth mindset means shedding limiting beliefs and fostering a strong mental framework that supports growth. This book will challenge you to think differently, set ambitious goals, and embrace the numerous possibilities that well-thought-out financial plans can offer.

Finally, today's world offers unprecedented tools and technology to aid your journey. From digital finance tools to online investment platforms, modern technology can be your ally in creating sustainable wealth. Each tool and strategy presented is tailored to inform and empower you, encouraging an interactive approach to wealth management where you are not just a spectator but an active participant.

Embarking on the quest for financial independence requires more than desire; it requires an actionable plan, resilience, and the courage to adapt and evolve. As you turn the pages, remember: wealth is within your grasp. Embrace the lessons, and you'll find that financial freedom isn't just an outcome but a lifestyle—one that's characterized by purpose, choice, and, above all, freedom.

Chapter 1:
Understanding Wealth

Understanding wealth begins with a mindset shift, one where you embrace the fact that wealth is more than just numbers in a bank account. It's about the freedom to make choices, pursue passions, and live life on your terms. Building wealth involves grasping the principles of financial independence and realizing how the psychology of money influences our decisions. By recognizing that wealth creation is a journey fueled by knowledge, informed decisions, and consistent actions, you lay the groundwork for a prosperous future. The most successful individuals are those who put in the effort to learn and apply financial strategies, transforming aspirations into real, tangible results. This chapter illuminates the critical foundation upon which lasting wealth is built, setting the stage for further exploration and mastery of personal finance in the chapters to come.

Defining Financial Independence

Achieving financial independence can feel like an elusive dream for many. It's the point where you no longer have to rely on a traditional paycheck to cover your expenses. Imagine waking up every morning with the freedom to pursue your passions, knowing that your financial needs are met through well-constructed income streams, savings, and investments. This isn't just about escaping the daily grind; it's about making choices unhindered by monetary constraints.

3

Financial independence isn't tied to age but to mindset and execution. It's about creating a life where money serves you, providing security, options, and time. To truly understand financial independence, one must first envision what it means personally. Some see it as early retirement, while others picture it as the ability to work when and where they want, on their own terms. The essence lies in having financial freedom, where your assets generate enough income to sustain your desired lifestyle without active employment.

Consider the traditional path: we work hard, save diligently, and hope to retire comfortably someday. However, the path to financial independence is a divergence from this conventional route, emphasizing asset accumulation, strategic investments, and financial literacy. One crucial distinction in this journey is the ability to generate passive income streams that sufficiently cover your living expenses.

Breaking down the concept further, financial independence demands a proactive approach to money management. It includes earning, saving, investing, and spending in ways that align with your long-term financial goals. This requires a shift from a consumerist mindset to one that values financial education and disciplined investing. Developing a robust financial plan is key, as it sets the pace and roadmap for your journey to independence.

A sturdy financial plan accounts for both anticipated and unforeseen expenses through prudent planning. This ensures that your core expenses, such as housing, healthcare, and daily living costs, are reliably covered. More than just having money, financial independence is about creating a safety net that supports you through life's unforeseeable events.

Having a clear understanding of your expenditure is essential. How much do you spend monthly on necessities, and more importantly, what share goes toward discretionary expenses? The clarity on these figures can guide you in setting a sustainable withdrawal rate, ensuring that your wealth outlives your needs. For most, achieving financial independence at an accelerated pace requires a strategic spending plan that trims the fat from their budgets, allowing more to be funneled into investments.

Investment plays a pivotal role in achieving financial independence. Savvy investors diversify their portfolios, spreading risk while leveraging opportunities in the stock market, real estate, and other asset classes. The goal is to make money work for you—not the other way around. With strategic investments, your wealth compounds over time, bringing the dream of financial independence closer.

Understanding the difference between assets and liabilities is foundational to this philosophy. An asset puts money in your pocket, whereas a liability takes money out. As you build your path to financial independence, focus on acquiring assets that will generate income, appreciate in value, or both. Reducing liabilities, such as consumer debt, simultaneously accelerates this process.

Remember, financial independence isn't just about the numbers. It's about peace of mind—the confidence that comes from knowing you're prepared for whatever life throws your way. This financial security catalyzes personal growth, allowing you more time and energy to invest in relationships, hobbies, and personal aspirations.

The journey to financial independence also involves cultivating the right mindset. It's about patience and perseverance, echoing the need to stay committed to your plan despite inevitable setbacks. Building a wealth mindset involves nurturing habits that reinforce financial disciplines, like regular saving, consistent investing, and prudent spending.

Beyond personal gains, achieving financial independence often paves the way for impacting others positively. When your financial house is in order, you can contribute more to community causes and support those around you. The freedom from financial worries enables a fuller, more enriched life experience while potentially fostering a spirit of generosity and philanthropy.

Ultimately, financial independence is a personal journey, distinct and individual for each of us. Yet, its definition remains consistent: the ability to make life choices without being overly constrained by financial concerns. It empowers you to craft the life you desire, equipping you to weather storms and embrace opportunities with equal vigor. So, as you envision your route to financial independence, remember: it's not just attainable, it's a journey worth the pursuit.

The Psychology of Money

To truly harness the power of wealth, you first need to understand your relationship with money. The way we think about money significantly influences our financial decisions and, ultimately, our financial independence. Money, in essence, isn't just paper or numbers on a screen; it's a powerful tool that reflects our values, emotions, and life experiences.

One of the most critical aspects of the psychology of money is our emotional attachment to it. Money can evoke a range of emotions, such as security, anxiety, or even freedom. For many, it's a source of comfort, ensuring that all basic needs are met. However, for others, it triggers stress and fear, especially when they're living paycheck to paycheck. Recognizing and acknowledging these emotions is the first step towards mastering your financial life.

Another core component of understanding the psychology of money is identifying personal beliefs about wealth. Often, these beliefs stem from childhood experiences and societal influences. If you grew up hearing that money is the root of all evil, you might shy away from pursuing wealth actively. On the other hand, if you learned that money enables you to help others, you might be more motivated to earn and manage it wisely. These ingrained beliefs can significantly impact your financial choices, sometimes without even realizing it.

To create lasting wealth, it's vital to challenge any negative money-related beliefs. If you believe wealth is unachievable, you might unconsciously sabotage your efforts toward financial independence. Start by reprogramming those beliefs. Understand that money, when managed wisely, can be a force for good that opens up opportunities and allows you to lead a more fulfilling life.

Consider the role of money in your self-worth and identity. Many people equate their wealth with their value as individuals. This mindset can lead to unhealthy habits, like overspending to impress others or fearing loss of status if their financial situation changes. By detaching your self-worth from your net worth, you empower yourself to make more rational and strategic financial decisions, free from the pressure of societal expectations.

Behavioral finance is an emerging field that sheds light on how psychological influences and biases affect financial behaviors. We often make irrational decisions due to cognitive biases like overconfidence, loss aversion, or herd mentality. For instance, overconfidence might lead an investor to gamble with risky stocks, believing they'll beat the market. Similarly, loss aversion might prevent someone from investing altogether, fearing they'll lose their hard-earned money.

To counter these biases, practice self-awareness and reflection. Take a moment to examine why you're making a particular financial decision. Is it based on sound data and logical reasoning, or is it driven by fear or the desire to keep up with others? Acknowledging these patterns can lead to better decision-making.

Another aspect of financial psychology involves understanding your spending habits. Are your purchases aligning with your long-term financial goals? Impulse buying and retail therapy might offer temporary satisfaction but can derail finances in the long run. Practicing mindful spending—where you consciously evaluate the necessity and value of each purchase—can be a game-changer. When you spend purposefully, you not only save money but also gain greater satisfaction from the things you do buy.

Likewise, cultivating an attitude of gratitude towards money can lead to better financial health. When you appreciate what you have, you're less likely to engage in comparison shopping or unnecessary spending. An attitude of abundance—believing there's plenty of wealth for everyone—encourages generosity and a willingness to share, instead of hoarding wealth out of fear.

Moreover, setting clear and motivating financial goals can transform your relationship with money. Goals shouldn't just be about accruing a certain amount but should reflect a deeper purpose, like financial security for your family or the ability to retire comfortably. When your goals resonate with your values, you're more likely to follow through on the actions needed to achieve them.

Developing the discipline to achieve financial goals involves both your mindset and habits. Discipline doesn't mean restriction; it's about consistently making choices that align with your aspirations. Whether it's sticking to a budget, saving regularly, or investing wisely, each step requires a blend of strategic thinking and emotional resilience.

Finally, remember that building wealth is as much about mindset as it is about numbers. Cultivating a positive, proactive attitude toward money can empower you to take control of your finances, make informed decisions, and create a future that truly reflects your dreams. It's not just about how much money you have, but how effectively you can harness your mindset and behavior to grow and maintain that wealth over time.

Chapter 2:
Mastering Personal Finance

Becoming proficient in personal finance is akin to crafting a solid foundation for a skyscraper—it's essential, not optional. It's about making your money work for you, ensuring every dollar has a purpose, and understanding that financial discipline is the bedrock of wealth creation. Though the journey to financial independence might seem daunting, embracing effective budgeting and debt management strategies can propel you forward. Crafting a realistic budget isn't just about limiting expenses; it's a way to prioritize what matters most and set the stage for larger financial victories. By mastering personal finance, you're not just surviving; you're setting sail towards a horizon filled with possibilities, armed with the knowledge and strategies to transform your financial destiny into one of abundance and security.

Budgeting for Success

In the grand journey of mastering personal finance, budgeting stands as a pivotal skill that forms the foundation for financial independence. It's more than just a series of calculations; it's about adopting a mindset that prioritizes intentional financial decisions. Creating a successful budget is like constructing a well-oiled machine. It's not just about tracking dollars and cents; it's about aligning your spending with your values and goals. With a strong budget, the pathway to financial success becomes clearer and more achievable.

First and foremost, understanding where your money goes is crucial. Begin by tracking your expenses for a month or two. This exercise might seem tedious at first, but it's a necessary step in gaining clarity over your financial habits. Discovering patterns in your spending can be eye-opening. Perhaps those small, frequent coffee purchases add up or maybe recurring subscriptions have been quietly draining your account. When you know where your money is going, you're equipped to make better decisions and adjust your habits as needed.

Once you've grasped your spending habits, categorizing your expenses into fixed and variable costs can be immensely helpful. Fixed costs—such as rent, insurance premiums, and utilities—are non-negotiable. However, variable costs, like dining out or entertainment, offer some flexibility. By identifying these areas, you can determine where to cut back when necessary. Making adjustments to variable expenses can free up funds to be directed towards savings or investments, aligning with your broader financial objectives.

A successful budget isn't just about cutting back; it's about deliberate allocation. The 50/30/20 rule provides a simple guideline: allocate 50% of your income to needs, 30% to wants, and 20% to savings and debt repayment. This framework is flexible and can be adjusted to suit your personal situation, but it's a solid starting point. Think of this not as a restriction, but as a way to empower yourself financially. The goal is to have the bulk of your money working for you, setting the stage for long-term growth and stability.

It's also critical to have a buffer for unforeseen expenses. Life is unpredictable and having a financial cushion can prevent setbacks from derailing your progress. This is where the concept of an emergency fund comes into play. While setting aside funds for emergencies might not be thrilling, it's a financial lifesaver. Aim to save at least three to six months' worth of expenses to cover any unexpected events, like a medical emergency or sudden job loss. This safety net ensures that unexpected challenges don't force you into debt or disrupt your financial plans.

Budgeting for success also involves setting clear financial goals. Whether it's paying off debts, saving for a home, or funding retirement, setting specific, measurable targets keeps you motivated and focused. When goals are in place, budgeting transforms from a mundane task into a strategic weapon designed to give you control over your future.

Revisiting and adjusting your budget regularly is as important as creating one. Life changes—the cost of living rises, incomes vary, and financial priorities shift. By revisiting your budget regularly, you allow for these changes, ensuring that your financial plan remains relevant and effective. It's helpful to sit down each month and assess whether you met your budget goals, and make adjustments as needed. Staying flexible with your budget helps to accommodate these shifts without causing panic or stress.

Technology can be a strong ally in your budgeting process. Numerous digital tools and apps can assist in managing your finances more effectively. From tracking expenses to sending alerts for due dates, these tools can simplify the process, allowing you to focus on bigger financial strategies. Leveraging technology enables you to automate savings and track spending on the go, making budgeting more accessible and less labor-intensive.

While budgeting may seem daunting to some, it's worth remembering that it's a means to an end. The aim is to achieve financial freedom and lessen the stress of living paycheck to paycheck. By crafting a budget that reflects your values and priorities, you open the door to a life where money is no longer a source of anxiety but a tool for building your legacy.

The journey to financial independence is much smoother when you're equipped with a robust budget. It provides clarity, control, and opportunities for growth. With discipline, dedication, and the right mindset, budgeting becomes not just a task, but a path to achieving the financial success you envision for your life. Embrace budgeting as your ally, and watch as it transforms your financial landscape into one of abundance and possibility.

Debt Management Strategies

When it comes to achieving financial independence, managing debt is one of the most pivotal steps you can take. Debt itself isn't inherently bad; it can sometimes be harnessed to your advantage. However, when it's mishandled, it becomes a significant barrier to wealth building, weighing down even the most astute saver. Let's explore strategies that will empower you to manage your debt, transform your financial habits, and set the stage for lasting prosperity.

Firstly, it's crucial to distinguish between good debt and bad debt. Good debt is an investment that will grow in value or generate long-term income, like student loans for higher education or a mortgage. Bad debt, on the other hand, typically refers to high-interest consumer debt such as credit cards that doesn't offer any return on investment. Recognizing the difference can inform your approach to paying it off expediently.

Before tackling your debt, perform a full assessment. List every one of your debts, no matter how small, along with their interest rates and minimum payments. Seeing your total debt picture can be daunting, but transparency is vital. This step ensures you have a clear understanding of where you stand and prevents any surprises down the road.

Next, create a plan focusing on one of the two main strategies: the Debt Snowball or Debt Avalanche method. The Debt Snowball method encourages you to pay off the smallest debts first, gaining momentum as each balance is eliminated. This tactic plays off psychological benefits, providing quick wins that can motivate further progress. Alternatively, the Debt Avalanche method prioritizes debts with the highest interest rates, thus minimizing your long-term financial charges. Choose the method that resonates with your personal motivation style and financial goals.

Once you've chosen your strategy, automate your payments wherever possible. Automation helps enforce discipline, ensuring you never miss a due date. It's a small step that can protect you from late fees and additional interest, allowing what you repay to focus on reducing the principal rather than penalty charges.

Enhance your repayment strategy by adjusting your lifestyle. This doesn't necessitate significant sacrifices; instead, consider mindful changes. Maybe that's brewing your coffee at home, canceling unused subscriptions, or negotiating better rates on utility bills. Every dollar saved can be an extra dollar towards your debt, expediting your journey to financial freedom.

Another crucial step is negotiating with creditors. It might seem daunting, but many people are surprised at how flexible loans and credit card terms can become with some dialogue. Request lower interest rates or inquire about financial relief programs. Creditors may be open to lowering your payments temporarily or even forgiving a portion of your debt if certain conditions are met.

Incorporate professional advice if your situation feels overwhelming. Credit counseling organizations offer resources and personalized plans to aid in debt management, often for free or at a low cost. They may also mediate on your behalf with creditors, consolidating payments into one easier-to-manage sum.

It's also wise to consider debt consolidation, which combines multiple debts into a single new one, preferably with a lower interest rate. This can simplify your payments and in some cases, reduce the interest you'll pay overall. However, do tread carefully; thorough research is needed to ensure the consolidation terms benefit you more than the original debts did.

As you're working through debt, build an emergency fund simultaneously. Even a small cushion can prevent you from piling on more debt when unexpected expenses arise. Regular, small contributions to this safety net can shield you from future setbacks, allowing your debt strategy to continue unabated.

Maintaining a positive mindset throughout this process is as important as the financial tactics themselves. Celebrate each debt repaid as an accomplishment and recognize how each step brings you closer to financial independence. Debt management is not only a financial journey but a transformative mindset shift that creates room for opportunities to thrive.

The road to mastering your personal finances is one that requires commitment and often, realignment of priorities. Debt, when managed wisely, doesn't have to be a scary specter looming over your financial future. Instead, it can be a stepping stone to mastering the art of personal finance. Embrace the challenge wholeheartedly and watch as you rewrite your financial story for good.

Chapter 3:
Saving Strategies for Growth

Navigating the path to financial independence requires a keen understanding of how to make every dollar work for you, and this is where saving strategies for growth come into play. It's not just about tucking money away; it's about harnessing its potential to create wealth. Begin by setting clear saving goals that align with your long-term vision, ensuring they are both ambitious and achievable. Prioritize establishing a robust emergency fund—this foundational step secures peace of mind and provides a buffer against unforeseen challenges. As you progress, the focus should shift to maximizing contributions to retirement accounts, taking full advantage of employer matches when available. This is your ticket to harnessing compound growth over time, turning small, consistent contributions into significant financial powerhouses. Remember, disciplined saving today lays the groundwork for tomorrow's opportunities, providing the momentum needed to transition from financial stability to financial growth. Embrace these strategies with a positive and proactive mindset, knowing that every step taken in saving is a step toward a future of abundance.

Emergency Funds Explained

Let's talk about one of the most underrated weapons in your financial arsenal: the emergency fund. An emergency fund isn't just a safety net; it's your personal buffer against life's unexpected hiccups. Imagine driving down a winding road without seat belts—risky, right? That's exactly what managing your finances without an emergency fund is like. It's risky business, and you certainly wouldn't want that kind of stress while striving for financial independence and lasting wealth.

The core purpose of an emergency fund is to cover unforeseen expenses like medical emergencies, car repairs, or sudden job loss without having to dip into your investments or savings set aside for other financial goals. It acts as a financial shock absorber, cushioning you from high-interest debt when an emergency strikes. But how much do you really need in such a fund? Financial experts often recommend having three to six months' worth of living expenses stashed away.

Your lifestyle, income stability, and financial obligations will heavily influence how much you need to save. If you're single in a stable career with no dependents, three months might suffice. Conversely, if you have a family or are self-employed, you might aim for a more robust six-month reserve. What's crucial is tailoring the fund to suit your unique circumstances and comfort levels.

Now, a common question pops up: "Where should I park my emergency fund?" Liquidity is key here. It should be easily accessible, yet far enough away to avoid the temptation of spending it for non-emergencies. High-yield savings accounts or money market accounts offer a good balance, providing some interest while keeping your funds readily available. While these options might not offer high returns, the goal here isn't wealth multiplication but immediate accessibility.

The journey to building an emergency fund might seem daunting at first, but it's achievable with the right strategy and discipline. Start by setting small, realistic savings goals. Begin with an initial target, maybe a month's worth of expenses, and gradually build up. Consider automating your savings where a portion of your paycheck is directly funneled into your emergency fund. This minimizes the temptation to use the money elsewhere and ensures consistent growth.

For many, reaching the full target of three to six months' worth of expenses might take time, and that's perfectly okay. What's important is starting and sustaining the momentum. Break down your objective into smaller, manageable parts, and each time you reach a milestone, give yourself a pat on the back. It will not only motivate you but also reinforce the positive habit of diligent saving.

We must also acknowledge the psychological comfort an emergency fund provides. Knowing that you've got a backup plan builds confidence. This peace of mind can positively influence other areas of financial planning. Without the lingering fear of "what if," you're likely to make calmer, more calculated decisions in your financial journey.

Nevertheless, filling your emergency fund isn't a one-time event. Life changes, and so should your fund. It's crucial to re-evaluate its size periodically, especially after major life changes like marriage, having a child, or changing jobs. Regular assessment ensures that your safety net remains suitable and robust.

Equally important is knowing when to replenish the fund. Upon dipping into it, prioritize restoring your emergency savings at the earliest opportunity. It's tempting to focus on other financial goals immediately afterward, but rushing to replenish your emergency savings fund helps maintain your prepared-for-anything stance.

Consider your emergency fund an enabler rather than a hindrance. Yes, it's money you're not investing or spending, but it safeguards your financial growth from unexpected detractors. By protecting your assets from depletion during emergencies, you allow your other investments to stay the course, harnessing the power of compound growth uninterrupted.

As daunting as it sounds, we're not alone in this journey. There's community, advice, and resources to draw from. Financial independence isn't built overnight, but each deliberate action, like starting an emergency fund, brings you a step closer. This financial cushion allows you the freedom to seek opportunities from a position of strength rather than desperation, and that's a victory in itself.

In summary, an emergency fund is a cornerstone of financial health and resilience. It guards against the unpredictable waves of life that can throw you off course, ensuring your aspirations for wealth and independence remain on track. By committing to this essential savings strategy, you're building a future that's not just wealthy but secure and stable. Read further to deepen your understanding and refine your savings strategies, as this forms the bedrock upon which true financial freedom stands.

Retirement Accounts Unveiled

Achieving financial independence involves more than just saving money—it's about making that money work for you, especially as you approach retirement. Retirement accounts are vital tools that help you achieve your vision of a financially secure future. With the right strategies, these accounts not just store value, but also fuel growth and wealth accumulation over time.

The magic of retirement accounts lies in their ability to leverage tax advantages. This can significantly accelerate your savings. For instance, contributing to an account like a 401(k) or a Traditional IRA lets you tuck away pre-tax dollars, reducing taxable income for the year. This is not just tax deferral; it's a strategic play, allowing your money to grow unhindered by annual tax liabilities. Compound interest becomes your ally, and as your account balances climb, your wealth-building momentum gains speed.

Now, not all retirement accounts are created equal, though. Each one comes wrapped with its own set of rules and benefits, and there's a remarkable freedom in this variety, letting you tailor your portfolio to meet your unique needs. A Roth IRA, for example, might be perfect for those expecting to be in a higher tax bracket later. You pay taxes on contributions today, but enjoy tax-free withdrawals in retirement. It's a choice with foresight, a testament to strategic planning.

Let's not forget the role of employer-sponsored retirement accounts. Many companies offer perks like matching contributions to 401(k) plans. When your employer matches your contributions, it's essentially free money deposited into your nest egg. It's a no-brainer to max out this benefit if it's offered. Matching programs can supercharge your savings trajectory, and neglecting them is like leaving money on the table.

Although the common names like IRA and 401(k) might dominate the conversation, other retirement savings vehicles deserve attention too. The SEP-IRA (Simplified Employee Pension) or a SIMPLE IRA (Savings Incentive Match Plan for Employees) offer excellent options for small business owners and the self-employed. These plans provide substantial annual contribution limits, offering flexibility and the potential for significant growth.

Consider how a Self-Directed IRA could change the game for savvy investors. Unlike traditional retirement accounts, the Self-Directed IRA unlocks doors to a wider range of investment opportunities, including real estate, precious metals, and private equity. This flexibility allows keen investors to leverage their expertise across diverse sectors, bringing their personal investment acumen into their retirement growth strategy.

No matter your choice, contributions alone aren't the holy grail of retirement planning. You need to be strategic about your withdrawal plan as well. Understanding required minimum distributions (RMDs) can prevent you from incurring hefty penalties and ensure your wealth stretches throughout retirement. For many, this stage of financial planning requires professional guidance, illuminating the importance of consulting a financial advisor to help finesse your strategy.

Automation can be a game-changer in maintaining discipline in contributions. Setting up automatic transfers from your paycheck to your retirement accounts ensures consistent growth without the monthly decision fatigue. It's a hands-off approach that harnesses the power of dollar-cost averaging, a technique which minimizes the impact of market volatility by maintaining consistent investments over time.

Thinking ahead, analyzing social security benefits, or considering annuities might also play key roles as additional layers in your retirement strategy. Diversifying income streams for retirement provides a hedge against unforeseeable market downturns or changes in personal circumstances.

Building a robust retirement portfolio is akin to navigating a well-defined journey, punctuated with strategic hustles and milestones. Each informed decision brings you closer to your goals of financial freedom. Empowered with knowledge, you pave the way toward a secure and fulfilling retirement, enjoying the fruits of years of smart, disciplined saving and investing.

The truth is, crafting your retirement strategy isn't just about the principles of saving but about seizing every opportunity to maximize future comfort and security. Equip yourself with knowledge, tap into every available resource, and invest with the understanding that your future-self will reap the rewards of today's strategic planning. In this way, your journey to retirement becomes less about sacrifice and more about smart choices shaping a wealth-filled future.

Chapter 4:
Investment Foundations

As you take the steps towards financial independence, understanding the foundational elements of investing becomes crucial. Investing isn't just a path to grow your wealth—it's about making your money work for you while you focus on living a fulfilling life. At its core, the world of investing offers a blend of opportunities and risks, and knowing the basics helps you navigate this landscape with confidence. Whether you're intrigued by the seemingly complex market dynamics of stocks and bonds or curious about the shared growth potential of mutual funds, the key is to understand the roles they play in building a diversified and resilient portfolio. By grounding yourself in these investment foundations, you can make informed decisions that align with your financial goals and set the stage for more advanced strategies. Embrace this knowledge as a stepping stone towards economic empowerment, and remember that each choice you make is a potential building block in your wealth creation journey. Invest wisely, and let your diligence set the course for prosperity.

Understanding Stocks and Bonds

There's a certain allure to the world of investing that captivates the imagination. For many, investing is the pathway to financial independence and a tool for wealth creation that promises empowerment and security. In the realm of investments, stocks and bonds stand as fundamental pillars. Understanding these instruments is crucial for anyone looking to establish a strong financial foundation.

Let's start with stocks. At their core, stocks represent ownership in a company. When you purchase a stock, you're essentially buying a piece of that company, no matter how small. This ownership stake means you get to share in the company's successes—and, yes, its failures. Owning stocks can be extremely rewarding, as companies grow and thrive. It's this potential for growth that draws investors in, offering the tantalizing possibility of substantial returns.

Bonds, by contrast, aren't about ownership. They represent a loan made by an investor to a borrower—usually a corporation or government. When you buy a bond, you're essentially acting as the lender. The borrower agrees to pay you interest over a specified period and to return the principal amount on the maturity date. Bonds are often seen as safer, more stable investments compared to stocks. They provide regular income through interest payments and are crucial for balancing an investment portfolio with some level of predictability.

Balancing stocks and bonds in an investment portfolio is akin to balancing risk and reward in life. Stocks, with their ownership element, often bring a higher level of risk but can offer substantial returns. Bonds, with their steady income, generally come with lower risk. This balance allows investors to navigate the unpredictable nature of markets, aiming for growth while safeguarding against potential downturns.

The risk associated with stocks varies significantly across different companies and industries. Blue-chip stocks, for instance, are shares in large, well-established companies with a history of reliable performance. They're typically less volatile and offer steady growth. On the other hand, growth stocks belong to companies expected to grow at an above-average rate compared to other companies. While they might not pay dividends, the potential for appreciation makes them attractive to investors looking for long-term growth.

Understanding the intricate dance between risk and reward is paramount when considering stocks and bonds. For stocks, it often involves evaluating a company's fundamentals, such as its revenue, profit margins, and growth potential. For bonds, understanding credit ratings and the issuer's financial health is key. This analysis helps investors determine where they want to allocate their resources based on their financial goals and risk tolerance.

Market conditions also play a crucial role in determining the attractiveness of stocks versus bonds. During periods of economic growth, stocks tend to perform well, as companies report higher earnings and investors are optimistic. Bonds might come to the forefront during economic slowdowns when stability is more coveted. This ebb and flow illustrate why diversification—spreading investments across various assets like stocks and bonds—is vital for risk management.

In general, the allocation between stocks and bonds could be guided by an investor's age, financial goals, and risk tolerance. Younger investors might lean more heavily towards stocks, aiming for long-term growth, while those nearing retirement might prefer the stability of bonds. However, there's no one-size-fits-all strategy. Investment decisions should be tailored to individual circumstances, keeping in mind the ultimate goal of financial independence.

The allure of investing in stocks and bonds doesn't just lie in potential returns. It's a journey of learning and development, an arena where you can witness the thrilling interplay between global events, business innovations, and financial news. Staying informed and maintaining a thirst for knowledge can turn this financial activity into a lifelong passion.

Whether you're drawn by the thrill of the stock market or the reliability of bonds, understanding these vehicles is a critical step on your journey towards financial empowerment. No matter where you begin, remember that investing is as much about patience and discipline as it is about profit. By mastering the basics of stocks and bonds, you lay the groundwork for a future where you're in control of your financial destiny.

Navigating Mutual Funds

Mutual funds offer a dynamic way to diversify your investment portfolio, a crucial step in laying a robust foundation for your financial future. Imagine entering a bustling marketplace where everyone wants what's best for their money. Here, mutual funds stand as a practical choice, managed by seasoned professionals who know how to navigate the financial waters. They pool your money together with that of other investors, creating a substantial fund that buys a diversified basket of stocks, bonds, or other securities, reducing your exposure to the ebbs and flows of the market.

Diversification is at the core of mutual funds, and it can't be emphasized enough. By investing in a single mutual fund, you're actually investing in a variety of assets. This spreads risk and can help stabilize returns over the long term. It's like enjoying a buffet of financial assets rather than sticking to just one dish. A well-diversified portfolio can withstand market volatility better than one that's heavily burdened on a single asset class. This strategy becomes particularly valuable when one segment of the market faces a downturn.

When choosing a mutual fund, you must consider your investment goals and risk tolerance. Are you aiming for growth, income, or a balanced approach? Answering this question helps narrow down the types of mutual funds that align with your objectives. Equity funds focus on stocks, aiming for growth; bond funds cater to income; and balanced funds deliver a mix of both, providing a more stable return over time. Understanding the types ensures you're aligned with what matters most to you financially.

Another factor to weigh is the fund's management style: active or passive. Active funds are like a custom-built house, where fund managers vigorously research and select securities, aspiring to beat market returns. They come with higher fees and the hope of greater rewards. On the other end, passive funds mirror a market index and usually offer lower fees, reflecting the efficiency of modern-day investment strategies. The choice between active and passive strategies depends largely on your market outlook and appetite for management fees.

Fees and expenses are quite significant in the world of mutual funds, impacting the overall return. Often invisible at first glance, they manifest through management expenses and load fees—an entry or exit cost for buying or selling funds. Compare various funds not just by their past performance but also by what costs you might incur. A lower-fee fund can substantially increase your returns over the long haul, similar to shopping smart by focusing on quality and price rather than just the price tag.

Many investors find mutual funds an attractive gateway to investment for their built-in convenience. They provide you with liquidity, allowing you to buy and sell shares easily and often without penalties, except in cases of early withdrawal in certain funds. This liquidity ensures you aren't locking your money away indefinitely, an often overlooked benefit when flexibility is a priority.

Before you make any investment, reviewing the fund prospectus is crucial. This document contains essential information about the fund's investment objectives, risks, performance, and management structure, acting as a road map. It's like getting to know the company you're about to partner with. Skipping this step is akin to agreeing to terms and conditions without reading them thoroughly—fundamentally flawed in nature and potentially costly in practice.

Consider the impact of economic factors and market trends on mutual fund performance. A fund's success is often tied to broader market dynamics, including interest rates, inflation, and geopolitical shifts. Staying informed about these factors helps you anticipate potential value changes in your mutual funds. This awareness doesn't mean you need to predict the future, but you should remain agile and prepared to adjust your positions as necessary.

Incorporating mutual funds into your investment strategy can also be a discipline. Use strategies like dollar-cost averaging—investing a fixed amount regularly regardless of market conditions. This approach minimizes the impact of market volatility and builds up your investment positions over time. By committing to a disciplined investment plan, you're more likely to avoid the common emotional traps that sabotage long-term financial growth. It's about consistency over the allure of timing the market.

Remember that while mutual funds offer diversified convenience, they're not a one-size-fits-all solution. Evaluating their fit within your broader investment portfolio is essential. Consider how they complement other investment vehicles like individual stocks, bonds, and real estate. A holistic view of your entire financial landscape ensures you're maximizing growth opportunities and managing risk effectively.

Finally, commit to ongoing education and evaluation of your mutual fund investments. The financial landscape is dynamic, and staying informed about changes within funds, or shifts in broader economic contexts, will help keep your strategy resilient. It's this ongoing commitment that transforms mere investment into sound wealth-building, paving the path to financial independence and, ultimately, a legacy of security and prosperity.

Chapter 5:
Advanced Investment Techniques

As we delve deeper into the realm of wealth building, it's time to explore advanced investment techniques that can transform your financial journey. These strategies are not just about adding new tools to your portfolio but about understanding and leveraging opportunities that many overlook. In this chapter, we'll uncover the nuances of investing beyond the traditional stocks and bonds. Real estate offers a tangible asset with potential for rental income and property appreciation, while alternative investments like commodities and cryptocurrencies present avenues for diversification and growth in a modern financial landscape. By embracing these sophisticated methods, you'll not only enhance your investment prowess but also strengthen your path toward lasting wealth and financial independence. Remember, it's about making informed decisions that align with your unique goals and risk tolerance. Let's think differently, act boldly, and move confidently toward a future where financial freedom isn't just a dream but a reality.

Real Estate Opportunities

Real estate—the very term conjures images of skyscrapers, quaint homes, bustling markets, and acres of land awaiting transformation. But beyond the physical structures and land, real estate represents one of the most dynamic avenues for wealth creation and investment. In the realm of advanced investment techniques, understanding these opportunities can propel aspiring investors toward financial independence.

Diving into real estate can seem daunting at first. It requires not only a keen eye for potential but also an understanding of the market, potential returns, and inherent risks. It's an investment vehicle where you can exercise considerable control over your investments. Unlike stocks, where you're essentially relying on a company's board and management, with real estate, the power is often in your own hands. Decisions you make can directly influence profitability, from choosing properties to manage and the renovations or upgrades to pursue.

One of the key attractions of real estate investment is cash flow. Rental properties, for example, continually generate income month after month. When managed effectively, a rental property can provide steady revenue that exceeds your monthly expenses, creating positive cash flow. This consistent income stream helps in covering costs, including mortgage payments, property management fees, insurance, and maintenance.

Besides regular income, real estate offers the advantage of property appreciation. Over time, property values tend to increase. While it's not guaranteed—and local market conditions can greatly influence this—historically, real estate has shown a tendency to appreciate in value, especially in developing regions or neighborhoods.

Leverage, in the context of real estate, is another compelling benefit. By using borrowed money, you can acquire more property than you could through cash purchase alone. This means greater potential returns as you're able to control a higher-value asset without committing the full value upfront. However, it's crucial to remember that leverage can also amplify losses, making risk management key.

Real estate investments also come with significant tax advantages. From deductions on mortgage interest and property taxes to the potential for tax-deferred gains through mechanisms like a 1031 exchange, the tax benefits can augment returns. It's advisable to work closely with a tax professional to ensure you're maximizing available benefits.

One way to ease into real estate is through Real Estate Investment Trusts (REITs). These allow you to invest in real estate without actually owning physical property. REITs are companies that own or finance income-generating real estate across a range of property sectors. They're bought and sold on major stock exchanges, similar to stocks, providing liquidity and reducing the barrier to entry for individuals interested in real estate.

Another strategy is flipping houses, which involves purchasing properties, often those needing TLC, renovating them, and selling at a profit. Although it can be lucrative, house flipping demands a solid understanding of the market, reliable contractor contacts, and an eye for true potential—what may seem profitable at first glance can sometimes lead to extensive unforeseen costs.

For those seeking stable returns, investing in rental properties might be the answer. Long-term rental properties can be a significant source of continuous income, especially in areas with strong demand. The challenge lies in identifying the right locations and ensuring property management is efficient to retain tenants and minimize vacancies.

The world of real estate isn't just limited to residential properties. Commercial real estate, including office buildings, retail outlets, and warehouses, provides another layer of opportunity. While the initial investment can be greater and the risk may seem heightened, the profit potential is often significantly larger as well.

As you explore real estate, networking remains a crucial component. Engage with other investors, join real estate investment groups, and perhaps find a mentor. These connections can offer support, share insights, and open doors to opportunities you might not find on your own.

Remember, the real estate market is cyclical. There'll be ups and downs. Riding the wave successfully requires patience, continuous learning, and adaptability. Keeping an eye on economic indicators, interest rates, and local market conditions will better position you to make informed decisions.

In sum, real estate offers diverse opportunities for wealth building. It's an arena where calculated decisions can lead to substantial gains, both in income and asset appreciation. While there are numerous strategies to explore, each comes with its own set of challenges and rewards. By tailoring your approach to match your risk tolerance, financial goals, and market understanding, you're setting the stage for success in this multifaceted field.

Exploring Alternative Investments

When it comes to building wealth and achieving financial independence, thinking outside the box can pay off significantly. Traditional investments like stocks, bonds, and mutual funds often take center stage, but there's a vibrant world of alternative investments that can diversify your portfolio and enhance your returns.

Alternative investments aren't just for the Wall Street elite or financial wizards. They've become increasingly accessible to everyday investors who are eager to explore opportunities beyond the conventional. From real estate to fine art, each alternative asset class offers its own unique set of characteristics, risks, and rewards. But why even consider alternative investments? It's simple—diversification is the cornerstone of any robust investment strategy.

Let's think about it for a minute. When you expand your investment horizon, you're essentially spreading your risk. The old adage "Don't put all your eggs in one basket" holds true. Alternative investments can act as a cushion during stock market downturns or periods of economic instability. They don't necessarily move in tandem with traditional markets, providing a hedge against potential losses.

Investing in real estate is often one of the first alternative investments people consider. It has tangible value, offers income potential through rentals, and can appreciate over time. Plus, there are several ways to get involved in real estate—from owning physical property to investing in Real Estate Investment Trusts (REITs).

But what if you're not interested in real estate? Well, the marketplace for alternative investments caters to diverse interests. Take private equity, for instance. It involves investing directly in private companies, often before they go public. Although this generally requires a more hands-on approach and a longer investment horizon, the potential returns can be substantial. Just think of being an early investor in a successful tech start-up!

For those with a taste for the finer things, collectibles such as fine art, wine, or classic cars can offer both personal enjoyment and financial growth. These investments often require specialized knowledge and a keen eye for value. What's fascinating is how these tangible assets can not only appreciate in value but can also offer a sense of satisfaction and personal fulfillment that stocks and bonds can't.

Venture capital is another enticing avenue. Here, you provide capital to startups or small businesses with high growth potential. Though these ventures carry significant risk—many startups fail to see their second birthday—the reward of being part of a breakthrough innovation is exhilarating and, potentially, highly lucrative.

Cryptocurrencies have also entered the scene as a controversial but undeniably transformative alternative investment. Investors are drawn to their decentralization and blockchain technology. Yet, the volatility of cryptocurrencies means they come with a high risk-reward ratio. Investing in this sphere requires a solid understanding of digital currencies and the technology behind them.

What about commodities like gold, silver, or even oil? These tangible resources often appeal to investors as a hedge against inflation. When the cost of living rises, commodities tend to hold or increase their value, balancing out losses in more volatile investments. This can be particularly reassuring in times of economic uncertainty.

Peer-to-peer lending platforms have also gained traction. They allow you to lend directly to individuals or businesses, cutting out the traditional banking middleman. While this can lead to better returns than a savings account, it's crucial to assess the credit risk involved, as borrowers can and do default.

However, it's essential to remember that alternative investments aren't immune to pitfalls. Markets can be less liquid, meaning you can't always sell them quickly. They might require specialized knowledge and involve higher fees. Doing thorough research and, if necessary, consulting with investment professionals can provide valuable insights to make informed decisions.

Alternative investments can ignite a spark of creativity in your wealth-building strategy. They challenge you to learn, to understand, and to adapt. As with any investment, due diligence is your best ally. Study the markets, honor your risk tolerance, and invest in what matches not just your financial goals but also your passions and interests. Alternative investments hold the power to not only diversify your portfolio but also to lead you on a path toward financial independence and lasting wealth.

Chapter 6:
Entrepreneurship as a
Wealth Pathway

Entrepreneurship offers a powerful avenue to financial freedom, inviting us to step into a realm where innovation meets opportunity. This path is not without its challenges, but the potential for wealth creation is transformative. By starting a venture, we leverage unique talents, create value, and generate income streams that can multiply over time. Scaling a business requires persistence, strategic thinking, and a keen understanding of market dynamics. For the determined, entrepreneurship is not just about financial gains—it's about building a legacy, influencing change, and realizing dreams. It's a journey that calls for grit and resilience, yet promises rewards beyond monetary wealth, turning visions into reality, and aspirations into tangible success.

Starting Your Own Business

Embarking on the journey of starting your own business is one of the most exhilarating paths you can take towards financial independence. It's a realm where your dreams can be transformed into reality, where your vision leads to tangible impact. But it's not just about the potential for financial success; it's about crafting a life on your terms, designing work that aligns with your values, and creating opportunities not only for yourself but for those around you.

Many of today's wealthiest individuals attribute their success to entrepreneurship. They've learned that starting and growing a business can be a powerful vehicle for wealth creation. Yet, the path isn't always straightforward. It demands resilience, strategic thinking, and a relentless pursuit of your goals. It's about seeing opportunities where others see obstacles, embracing risks, and a willingness to learn and adapt.

The first step in starting your own business is identifying your passion and assessing its potential in the marketplace. Passion fuels persistence, and your enthusiasm becomes contagious, inspiring others to believe in your vision. However, passion alone won't pay the bills. Market research is critical to ensure your idea has the potential to meet a need or solve a problem. Look at current industry trends, understand your target audience, and scrutinize your competition to carve out a unique niche for your business.

Once you've identified a viable business idea, crafting a solid business plan is essential. This document serves as your roadmap, detailing your business goals, marketing strategies, financial forecasts, and operational plans. It helps you define your business structure, whether it be a sole proprietorship, partnership, LLC, or corporation, and lays the groundwork for strategic growth. A thorough plan not only guides you but it also communicates your vision and strategy to potential investors and stakeholders.

Funding your business venture is another critical step. There are various avenues to explore, from bootstrapping with personal savings to seeking out investors or applying for business loans. Consider what aligns best with your goals and willingness to share ownership or responsibility. Whichever path you choose, managing finances prudently from the outset sets the foundation for long-term stability and growth.

Building a strong brand is essential in distinguishing your business in a crowded marketplace. Think of your brand as the personality of your enterprise, encompassing your message, tone, and visual identity. A well-developed brand resonates with consumers, fostering trust and loyalty. Utilize digital marketing tools to create and maintain an online presence that reflects your brand's values and engages your audience effectively.

Successful entrepreneurs understand the importance of surrounding themselves with the right people. Assembling a team that shares your vision and complements your skills is crucial. Hiring employees who bring different strengths and perspectives can propel your business forward. Remember, while you may be the visionary, your team often turns that vision into reality through dedication and execution.

From legal considerations and licenses to setting up efficient operations, the nuts and bolts of starting a business can seem daunting. Delving into the logistics, such as securing permits or setting up accounting systems, may not evoke the same excitement as developing your big idea, but they're vital aspects of building a robust architecture for success.

The timing of scaling your operations is a delicate balance in startup life. Weighing demand against capacity involves careful assessment. Rushing growth can overextend resources, while delaying expansion might mean missed opportunities. Analyzing metrics like customer feedback and financial performance helps in deciding when and how to scale, ensuring that growth is sustainable.

To stay relevant and competitive, continuous innovation must be part of your company's ethos. Adapting to changes in technology, economic shifts, and customer preferences is not only necessary for survival but for thriving in business. Encourage a culture of creativity among your team, where new ideas are welcomed and scrutinized for potential enhancement of your services or products.

Entrepreneurship is not merely a wealth pathway; it's a journey rich in personal and professional rewards. The freedom to make decisions, to pivot and innovate, and to align your work with your personal principles is invaluable. As you set forth on this exciting path, remember that every challenge is a chance to learn, and every success is a milestone in the magnificent tapestry of your entrepreneurial journey.

Ultimately, the journey of starting your own business is about taking ownership of your future, capitalizing on your unique talents and passions, and striving to leave an impact. The road may be fraught with challenges, but with perseverance, strategic planning, and a passion to succeed, you can craft a legacy that endures for generations.

Scaling Your Enterprise

In the journey of entrepreneurship, starting a business is just the beginning. Scaling your enterprise is where transformative growth occurs, and the transition from a small operation to a significant player in your industry happens. To achieve this, one must harness the right strategies, resources, and mindsets. Scaling isn't merely about expanding your business size; it's about expanding your impact, increasing efficiency, and maximizing profitability. It involves replicating a successful blueprint on a larger scale and doing so sustainably.

Building a strong foundation is key. Without a strong base, any growth is precarious. Consider your business model as the root system of a tree; it must be robust enough to support substantial growth. This necessitates a solid understanding of your market, a well-defined value proposition, and efficient operation processes. If these elements are not already in place, they should become your priority before seeking growth. As you strengthen your foundation, reflect on your business's core capabilities and scalability. Are your processes flexible enough to handle increased demand without compromising quality?

Once the foundation is solid, you should focus on enhancing operational efficiency. This often requires investing in technology and process automation to streamline operations and reduce manual workloads. Technology isn't just about flashy gadgets; it's a vital component for scaling. Automate repetitive tasks where possible, and utilize data analytics to make informed decisions. By reducing the time spent on routine tasks and improving accuracy, you free up resources to focus on strategic growth initiatives rather than operational headaches.

But scaling isn't just a matter of mechanics and logistics; it's equally about adapting your mindset. As a leader, seeing the bigger picture and delegating responsibilities is crucial. You need to build a team that's not just capable but also passionate about the vision of the company. The dynamics of a small business change significantly when you're scaling. Leaders must transition from doing everything themselves to trusting others to carry out their vision. Strong communication and setting clear objectives become vital. After all, a business is only as powerful as the team behind it.

Furthermore, financing is a significant component of the scaling equation. It's imperative to secure sufficient capital to support growth initiatives. Whether through reinvested profits, loans, or attracting investors, having an appropriate financial strategy ensures that scaling efforts do not overextend your resources. Maintaining positive cash flow while managing risks is crucial. Smart entrepreneurs will foresee potential financial risks and establish financial safeguards to keep their enterprise secure as it expands.

Part of the scaling process also involves amplifying your customer base. A deeper understanding of your target audience and tailoring your marketing efforts to reach new and existing customers more effectively is essential. With a clear brand message and targeted campaigns, you can establish a loyal customer base that supports your growth. Remember, it costs significantly more to acquire new customers than to retain existing ones, so building loyalty should be a priority.

In parallel, partnerships and networking play a crucial role in scaling your business. Collaborations can fuel growth by providing access to new markets, additional resources, and shared expertise. Leveraging partnerships allows you to offer more comprehensive solutions to your customers, enhancing your value proposition. Don't underestimate the power of a strategic alliance; the right partner can be a catalyst for change.

Moreover, as you scale, maintaining your business's culture becomes a priority. Rapid growth can disrupt established cultures, potentially leading to a disconnect between your team and your business's core values. Investing in your team's development and maintaining a positive work environment nurtures innovation and retention. Your employees are likely the strongest advocates of your brand, and their alignment with your business's mission is crucial for sustained growth.

Finally, measuring success through relevant metrics is paramount. You need to track your progress meticulously to ensure that your growth strategies are effective. Quantitative data like sales growth, profit margins, and customer acquisition costs are important, but qualitative insights such as customer satisfaction and employee engagement can offer a more rounded view of your business health. Having a regular review process ensures you can pivot quickly if certain strategies aren't producing the desired outcomes.

Scaling a business isn't an overnight endeavor, nor is it a one-size-fits-all process. It requires a blend of strategic planning, resourcefulness, and perseverance. As you navigate this complex journey, remember that each step forward brings you not only closer to your goals but also solidifies your path to financial independence and lasting wealth. The stories of successful entrepreneurs aren't just tales of expansion; they're narratives of resilience, innovation, and the relentless pursuit of making a difference.

Scaling allows you to leverage what you've built to impact broader markets and ultimately achieve your grander vision. So embrace the challenges, learn from them, and use them as stepping stones to elevate your enterprise to new heights.

Chapter 7:
Cultivating a Wealth Mindset

To truly cultivate a wealth mindset, you've got to embrace a new way of thinking that transforms your vision of financial freedom into reality. Start by recognizing that your beliefs about money are the foundation of your financial destiny. A mindset open to growth views challenges as opportunities, nurturing the resilience needed to overcome setbacks. Break free from limiting thoughts that whisper 'it can't be done' and replace them with a confident 'how can I achieve this?' Visualize your financial goals with clarity and commitment, knowing that unwavering focus can turn dreams into assets. Building wealth isn't just about what you accumulate but the quality of the financial decisions you make along the journey. Equip yourself with a dynamic approach, embrace continuous learning, and stay adaptable to shifts in the economic landscape. This mindset isn't about making a quick buck; it's about laying the groundwork for a future that's secure and prosperous, one intentional choice at a time. Lean into action and let your purposeful steps redefine your financial future.

Overcoming Mindset Barriers

Cultivating a wealth mindset isn't just about financial knowledge and investment strategies. At its core, developing a wealth mindset requires breaking through psychological barriers that have held you back from achieving financial independence. These barriers are often deeply ingrained beliefs about money, success, and personal worth that might have been developed in childhood. Addressing these beliefs isn't just a matter of understanding them—it's about transforming them into positive affirmations that propel you toward your financial goals.

Firstly, one of the most persistent barriers is the fear of failure. Many of us have been conditioned to view failure as an end point, rather than a stepping stone. However, embracing failure as a part of the learning process is critical in building a wealth mindset. Instead of letting past mistakes paralyze you, use them as launchpads for future success. It's about understanding that each setback is actually an opportunity to gather insights, refine strategies, and grow stronger.

Closely tied to the fear of failure is the fear of success. You might not immediately recognize this fear, but it can manifest in self-sabotaging behaviors. For instance, you might subconsciously resist taking bold financial steps because success brings change, and with change comes uncertainty. The fear of alienating friends or losing a sense of identity can also accompany this fear. To overcome this, it's important to visualize success in a positive light; imagine not just the material benefits, but also how you can impact others positively along the way.

When we talk about shifting mindsets, self-worth plays a crucial role. Many struggle with the idea that they're "not worthy" of wealth. This belief can limit your ambitions and stunt your growth. Start by acknowledging your value and dismantling any narratives that suggest you're less deserving. Remember, financial abundance doesn't discriminate—it's about recognizing opportunities and believing you're capable and worthy of seizing them. Cultivating a sense of self-worth helps lay the foundation for confident financial decisions.

Another pervasive barrier is the mindset of scarcity. This mindset operates on the belief that there's not enough wealth to go around, which in turn fosters competition and anxiety. Transitioning to an abundance mindset changes your focus from competition to

Np Chambers

collaboration. Recognize that sharing knowledge and resources can lead to mutual growth. When you operate from abundance, you become open to opportunities that you might have overlooked in a scarcity state of mind.

Perfectionism can be another stealthy hindrance. While striving for excellence is admirable, the pursuit of perfection can prevent you from taking action. In wealth building, waiting for the "perfect" moment or the "ideal" opportunity might cause you to miss out on substantial gains. Accept that no investment or strategy is flawless or without risk. It's about making informed decisions and being willing to make adjustments along the way.

Building a support network is also vital in overcoming these mindset barriers. Surround yourself with individuals who inspire and challenge you. Engage with communities or mentors who have achieved what you're aiming for—they can provide valuable insights that accelerate your journey. A supportive and knowledgeable network not only offers encouragement but also helps normalize wealth-building aspirations, making them more tangible and achievable.

History and society shape a lot of overall financial anxieties. For some, there can be intergenerational notions of financial limits or ceilings. Overcoming these barriers involves shifting the narrative from one of limitation to one of possibility. This isn't just a mental exercise; it involves actively seeking knowledge and implementing practices that demonstrate progress, however small. Experiment with new financial strategies and monitor your growth—it's these small wins that gradually defuse perceived limitations.

Finally, cultivating a wealth mindset requires patience and perseverance. Changing deeply rooted beliefs takes time and effort. Financial independence isn't about sudden transformations, but the gradual shift in how you perceive and interact with money. Practice mindfulness and reflection regularly to remain aware of your progress

42

and setbacks, adjusting your course as needed. Celebrate each milestone on your journey as proof that your mindset is indeed evolving towards one of wealth and abundance.

In overcoming mindset barriers, you carve out a path to financial freedom that is not just achievable but sustainable. Recognizing and transforming these psychological hurdles enables you to navigate wealth-building strategies with confidence and resilience. In doing so, you unlock the potential to realize goals beyond material wealth—opening doors to personal growth and a more fulfilling life.

The Power of Financial Goals

The journey toward financial independence is like navigating a vast, uncharted sea. While the destination is tantalizingly clear—freedom from financial worry and the security of a prosperous future—getting there requires more than just a wish or a vague plan. It demands the sharp compass of well-defined financial goals. Imagine financial goals as the stars guiding your ship through the night; they're not just milestones but lighthouses beaming you toward your ultimate destination of wealth.

Establishing financial goals provides clarity and direction. It transforms idle dreams into actionable plans. Without goals, you're adrift, susceptible to every financial wave or storm that comes your way. Yet, with solid, clear goals, you build resilience. You're empowered to chart a deliberate course, ensuring you're consistently moving toward your vision of financial independence. The act of goal-setting infuses your wealth-building strategies with purpose and precision.

Financial goals act as a framework for making wise decisions. When faced with choices—should you invest in stocks or start a savings account, should you buy that new gadget or save for property—the goals you've set provide a litmus test. They help streamline decision-making, stripping away distractions and focusing your efforts on actions that are aligned with your larger aspirations. This approach saves both time and resources, ensuring that your efforts remain productive and purposeful.

But what makes a financial goal effective? It begins with clarity. Vague goals like "I want to be rich" lack the power needed to spur action. Instead, aim for specifics. Consider goals like, "I want to save $10,000 for an emergency fund within the next year," or "I plan to eliminate all credit card debt in the next 24 months." These detailed aspirations naturally foster accountability and allow for measurable progress.

Equally important is the attainability of your goals. Lofty ambitions are commendable, but they must remain realistic within the bounds of your current financial situation and foreseeable opportunities. This doesn't mean stifling ambition but rather acknowledging the incremental steps required along the path to wealth. By setting achievable targets, you maintain motivation and gather momentum as each minor victory propels you forward.

Financial goals are also dynamic and should grow alongside you. As your financial situation evolves—perhaps through increased income or changing expenses—your goals need to be flexible. Reassess them regularly to ensure they reflect your current ambitions and the shifts in your circumstances. Periodic reviews will keep you aligned with your long-term vision, allowing for necessary recalibrations while maintaining forward momentum.

But what's truly transformative is the psychological impact of setting and achieving financial goals. It nurtures a sense of discipline and sharpens your focus, key traits in overcoming mindset barriers. With each goal you achieve, your confidence swells, reinforcing the belief that financial independence is within reach. This cycle of setting, achieving, and resetting goals builds a powerful psychological momentum, propelling you ever closer to lasting wealth.

A vital tool in this process is visualization. Envision what reaching your financial goals will mean for you and your life. Picture the freedom, the security, the opportunities that financial success will unlock. This vision becomes a powerful motivator, driving you toward disciplined action even on days when the progress seems slow or the obstacles feel daunting.

Moreover, financial goals promote long-term thinking. By compelling you to look beyond immediate gratification, they help shift your focus from short-term spending to long-term investing and saving. This shift in perspective is crucial in cultivating a mindset where future gains become more compelling than instant rewards. It's in this arena of patient, disciplined effort that wealth is truly built.

To make goals comprehensive, consider categorizing them. Short-term goals, like saving for a vacation within the year, keep motivation high with quick wins. Mid-term objectives, such as paying off a significant chunk of student loans, stabilize your financial ground. Long-term goals, such as building a retirement fund or purchasing investment property, secure your financial future. Each category plays a unique role in your financial strategy, converging to form a robust and balanced financial life.

Accountability is another cornerstone of achieving financial goals. Sharing your goals with a trusted friend, financial advisor, or community provides an external layer of motivation. This network can offer support, insights, and gentle nudges if you stray from your path. Also, tracking your progress regularly can keep the momentum alive, providing tangible proof of your efforts and successes.

Remember, setbacks are a natural part of this journey. They shouldn't deter you from pursuing your goals. Instead, view them as opportunities for learning and growth. Understand why a particular goal wasn't met on time and adjust your strategies accordingly. This adaptability is key to maintaining a wealth mindset and ensuring continued progress, even in the face of obstacles.

In essence, financial goals are not static roadmaps—they're evolving blueprints for your future. They ignite action, foster resilience, and provide clarity, making them indispensable elements in the pursuit of wealth. By consistently redefining these goals to match your evolving circumstances and aspirations, you position yourself to navigate the complexities of finance with dexterity and determination.

Your financial goals are more than numbers or timelines—they are a testimony to your commitment to a prosperous future. Embrace them with dedication, adapt them with purpose, and let them drive you toward the financial independence and lasting wealth you dream of achieving.

Chapter 8:
Risk Management in Wealth Building

Building wealth isn't just about accumulation; it's about preservation too. Successful wealth builders know that managing risk is as important as seeking returns. This chapter explores the vital tools and strategies necessary for safeguarding your financial future, weaving in principles that are both motivational and instructional. To truly thrive, one must be proactive in protecting the assets painstakingly cultivated over time. The art of risk management encompasses understanding potential threats and implementing robust safety nets, including various forms of insurance designed to buffer against unforeseen events. These measures not only secure what's already achieved but also allow for bolder financial moves, knowing that the foundation is solidly protected. In the journey toward financial independence, embracing a mindset that prioritizes asset protection and foresees potential pitfalls can be the difference between enduring wealth and unforeseen setbacks. Let this serve as a reminder that taking the right precautions today equips you for greater opportunities tomorrow.

Protecting Your Assets

When it comes to building and maintaining wealth, safeguarding what you have is just as vital as growing it. After all, your journey toward financial independence would be futile if you don't protect your assets from unforeseen risks that can undermine years of hard work and savvy planning. Think of asset protection as the foundation upon which the future of your wealth is built. Without a solid foundation, even the grandest of structures can crumble under pressure.

First and foremost, asset protection involves recognizing potential risks and implementing strategies to mitigate them. We're not just talking about physical assets like property and cash but also intangible ones, including intellectual property and investment accounts. Unpredictable events—like market downturns, legal challenges, or even personal liabilities—can hit when least expected. Knowing these challenges can surface at any moment prepares you to respond effectively and prevent significant losses.

For a start, diversifying your investments can serve as a sturdy shield against financial setbacks. Diversification, in essence, means not putting all your proverbial eggs in one basket. By allocating your investments across various asset classes, such as stocks, bonds, and real estate, you minimize the impact of any sector-specific turbulence. A well-diversified portfolio can withstand the ups and downs of market cycles, guarding your wealth against unnecessary risks.

Moreover, setting up legal structures like trusts can go a long way in safeguarding your investments. Trusts not only offer privacy and confidentiality but also provide a layer of protection against lawsuits and creditors. By placing your assets in a trust, you ensure they are handled according to your wishes while shielding them from potential legal disputes. Remember, it's not about avoiding your obligations but rather organizing your assets in a way that keeps them insulated from unwarranted claims.

Beyond trust structures, consider entity formation for businesses as a way to protect personal wealth. Forming limited liability companies (LLCs) or corporations can separate your personal assets from business liabilities. This separation means that, if your business encounters financial difficulties, your personal wealth remains protected. It's a strategic move that allows entrepreneurs to take calculated risks without jeopardizing personal finances.

In addition to structural protections, making wise choices in insurance coverage is crucial. Insurance acts as your financial safety net, absorbing costs during unexpected life events. From homeowner's insurance that covers property theft and damage to comprehensive health insurance that mitigates medical expenses, having the right mix of coverage can mean the difference between a minor setback and a financial catastrophe. Regularly reviewing and adjusting your policies ensures they continue to meet your evolving needs.

Furthermore, don't overlook the importance of estate planning. Asset protection isn't just about preserving wealth during your lifetime but also ensuring its seamless transition to the next generation. Crafting a comprehensive estate plan with wills, healthcare directives, and powers of attorney helps dictate how your assets will be managed and distributed. Such foresight not only sidesteps potential family disputes but also minimizes the tax burdens on your heirs.

Technology, too, plays a transformative role in asset protection. In today's digital world, it's critical to safeguard your financial data from cyber threats. Utilizing strong passwords, enabling two-factor authentication, and keeping software updated are fundamental practices in protecting sensitive information. As cyber-attacks become increasingly sophisticated, prioritizing digital security is no longer optional; it's essential.

Now, asset protection isn't a one-time effort but rather an ongoing process demanding active management. Regularly assessing and adjusting your strategies as your life circumstances and financial goals evolve is paramount. Professional advice from financial advisors, legal experts, and insurance agents can offer insights you might have missed and keep your strategies aligned with current regulations and market conditions.

On a broader level, fostering a mindset of due diligence and responsibility is key. By consistently living below your means and avoiding unnecessary debts, you not only protect your current assets but also create a buffer that smooths out any financial turbulence. Prudence entails having an emergency fund that caters to unforeseen expenses, ensuring that you don't dip into long-term investments or disrupt your wealth-building momentum.

Your assets represent the fruits of your labor and the manifestations of your ambitions. Treating them with the care and protection they deserve is a commitment to your financial future. As you continue your journey towards wealth building, let asset protection be the vigilant guardian that stands by your side, enabling you to face any challenge with confidence and perseverance.

In conclusion, the path to financial independence is strewn with both opportunities and risks. By being proactive in protecting your assets, you lay the groundwork for enduring success and stability. Let these strategies empower you to forge ahead with resolve, knowing that your wealth has a strong protective shield, ready to take on whatever the future may hold.

Insurance and Financial Safety Nets

In the quest for financial independence and robust wealth-building strategies, risk management takes center stage. It's easy to get caught up in the excitement of investments and income generation, but neglecting the safety nets can sometimes lead to painful setbacks. Imagine spending years building wealth, only to see it crumble due to an unexpected event. That's where insurance and financial safety nets come into play.

Insurance serves as a protective shield against the unpredictability of life. It helps ensure that regardless of what comes your way, your financial journey remains uninterrupted. Different types of insurance address various aspects of life and business, each crucial in maintaining a steady financial footing. For instance, health insurance covers medical expenses, safeguarding against the hefty costs of healthcare. Similarly, life insurance provides for your loved ones in your absence, ensuring their financial security.

Beyond the basics, there are other policies designed to cover specific types of risks. Homeowners insurance protects one of your most significant assets—your home—against damage or theft. Likewise, auto insurance covers your vehicles against accidents, theft, and liability. These are more than just policies; they're essential elements of a comprehensive risk management strategy.

Think of insurance premiums not as costs, but as investments in peace of mind. It allows you to take calculated risks elsewhere, knowing you've got a fallback. The key is finding the right balance between adequate coverage and affordable premiums. It's often tempting to skimp on insurance to save money, but doing so can leave you vulnerable. The investment in a reliable safety net now can save you from financial devastation later.

Another aspect to consider is disability insurance. It often goes overlooked, yet it's critical. Your ability to earn an income is one of your greatest assets. Disability insurance ensures you can continue meeting financial obligations if you become unable to work due to illness or injury. This type of insurance provides a safety net not only for you but for anyone dependent on your livelihood.

It's important to periodically reassess your insurance needs. Life changes—such as marriage, the birth of a child, or purchasing a home—can significantly affect your coverage requirements. As your wealth grows, adjusting your policies ensures they're aligned with your current financial situation, offering continued protection as your assets and responsibilities expand.

The next layer of protection lies in establishing financial safety nets beyond insurance. An emergency fund, for instance, functions as a financial buffer, offering liquidity in times of crisis. Ideally, this fund should cover three to six months of living expenses. It's there to prevent you from dipping into your investments or going into debt when unexpected expenses arise.

Furthermore, diversifying income sources is another strategic safety net. Chapter 9 discusses building multiple income streams, an essential tactic for maximizing financial stability. Combining insurance, savings, and income diversification crafts a multi-layered defense, ensuring financial security in a variety of circumstances.

We can't overlook the role of legal safeguards in protecting financial gains. Asset protection strategies involve structuring your assets in a way that shields them from creditors or lawsuits. Trusts and limited liability companies (LLCs) are common tools used for this purpose. While these may seem complex, engaging with financial advisors and legal professionals can provide clarity and guidance.

Ultimately, the aim is to create a resilient portfolio that stands strong amidst life's challenges and uncertainties. Building wealth isn't just about making money; it's about keeping it and ensuring it grows consistently. Insurance and financial safety nets are indispensable allies in this pursuit. They empower you to take bold steps in wealth-building, knowing that while risks abound, you're meticulously prepared for whatever lies ahead.

In summary, don't underestimate the importance of these protective measures. They are the unsung heroes of wealth management, fortifying your journey towards financial independence. By weaving insurance and financial safety nets into your strategy, you not only mitigate risks but also pave a smoother path to long-term prosperity.

Chapter 9:
Building Multiple Income Streams

Achieving financial independence isn't just about working harder; it's about working smarter by diversifying your income streams. Picture each stream as a safety net that catches you when life's unexpected twists occur. While an unwavering job might seem like a fortress, relying solely on one paycheck limits both potential and security. Creating multiple streams can start with something as straightforward as exploring passive income opportunities or investing time in side hustles, where your passions meet profitability. As you cultivate these streams, you'll build a robust financial ecosystem capable of weathering economic storms and seizing unexpected opportunities. It's this strategic diversification that transforms financial stability into financial freedom, allowing you to thrive rather than merely survive. Embrace the journey of diversification, for each step taken expands your horizons and brings the goal of financial independence within reach.

Passive Income Ideas

In a world where financial independence is increasingly intertwined with the freedom to live life on your terms, passive income can feel like a beacon of hope. Imagine the comfort in earning money while you sleep, allowing you to focus on what truly matters—family, passion projects, hobbies, or even philanthropic endeavors. But let's clarify: passive income doesn't mean zero effort. It requires foresight, strategic planning, and occasionally, a bit of sweat equity. With the right approach, though, this income stream can become a cornerstone of your wealth-building journey.

Real estate investment is one of the most popular paths to generating passive income. The idea of owning property and collecting rental income is alluring, and for good reason. With long-term appreciation of property values, coupled with the consistent monthly income from tenants, real estate offers dual benefits. First, identify a property in a location with solid growth potential. Ensure the financials work in your favor by calculating expenses and potential returns meticulously. Sometimes, the real challenge is finding the right tenants, maintaining property, and handling unforeseen expenses. But, overcoming these challenges results in a reliable income stream that can weather economic fluctuations.

Dividend stocks also deserve a spot on any list of passive income ideas. This income strategy involves investing in stocks that regularly distribute a portion of the company's earnings back to shareholders. It requires some initial capital and a careful assessment of stocks known for stable dividend payouts. The beauty lies in the compounding effect—reinvesting dividends can significantly boost your investment portfolio over time. Spend time researching companies with a strong track record of performance and dividend growth. While market fluctuations exist, dividends from mature, financially sound companies can provide a reassuring source of regular income.

For those looking to harness the digital revolution, creating and selling digital products can be both lucrative and fulfilling. Think online courses, e-books, or even membership sites. Initially, you'll invest time creating quality content that's educational, entertaining, or uniquely valuable. Platforms like Udemy or Teachable can host your course, while Shopify or Amazon handle e-book distribution. Once the product is live, sales can trickle in autonomously. Marketing efforts can amplify results, but the core promise of passive income remains intact.

Consider peer-to-peer lending as another viable option. This involves lending money to individuals or businesses through online services that facilitate these transactions. By acting as a lender, you can earn interest on loans. This modern twist on traditional lending has gained traction as fintech platforms provide unprecedented access to a wide pool of borrowers and lenders globally. While this avenue does carry risk—borrower default, market-risk variations—diligent research and portfolio diversification can mitigate potential downsides.

Writing a book, either fiction or non-fiction, can pave the way for another passive income stream. Sure, it requires creativity, perseverance, and initial support. But once published, each sale contributes to ongoing income. Self-publishing platforms like Amazon Kindle Direct Publishing simplify the process, allowing authors to retain more control and a larger share of royalties. Test your ideas first; maybe even run a blog that gauges reader interest and hones your writing skills. A well-received book can transform into more than its initial revenue—it can open doors to speaking engagements, consulting opportunities, or even expanded franchises.

Another creative avenue is photography. Selling stock photos online can be a great way to monetize your skills and passions. Websites like Shutterstock and Adobe Stock allow photographers to upload images and earn royalties whenever someone buys or downloads them. The focus here should be on quality and diversity—fresh, relevant, and high-resolution photos that meet market demands. The upfront time investment might seem daunting, but the allure of earning money while cultivating your art form makes it an appealing option.

Investing in REITs (Real Estate Investment Trusts) is a more liquid alternative to directly owning property. By purchasing shares in a REIT, you effectively own a slice of a portfolio of real estate assets managed by professionals. REITs often pay substantial dividends, offering a steady income stream with reduced individual asset management stress. They're suited for those who want exposure to real estate without the burdens of property management or substantial capital requirements. Always seek to understand the specific market sectors each REIT focuses on, be it commercial, residential, retail, or industrial, aligning with your financial goals.

Venturing into affiliate marketing offers a low-cost, flexible means of earning passive income online. As an affiliate marketer, you promote products or services through your blog, website, or social media, earning a commission for each sale or lead generated through your links. The key is authenticity—choosing products that align with your brand and resonate with your audience. While success requires upfront work on content creation and audience building, the rewards can be substantial once your system is well-oiled.

Digital advertising through platforms like Google AdSense or website banners can also generate passive income. If you already maintain a website or blog with significant traffic, monetizing it through advertisements can be seamless. Focus on producing quality content to attract visitors and engage them. The number of visitors clicking your ads translates directly to income, creating a virtuous circle of content creation and monetization.

Building passive income streams requires an understanding of your risk tolerance, initial capital, abilities, and existing knowledge base. Start small if needed—diversifying over time allows for steady growth without overwhelming yourself. Remember, there's no magic formula to immediate success, but consistent efforts compound incrementally into substantial passive income. And this isn't just about money; it's about creating a life where you control your time and decisions, ultimately living a life of purpose and intention.

The journey to financial independence isn't just for the select few who have cracked the code but for anyone willing to learn, adapt, and persist. Each passive income journey is personal, weighted by individual choices and circumstances. So explore, pilot, and perfect the pathways that feel natural, and soon enough, you'll find your portfolio blossoming into a reliable source of passive income.

Side Hustles for Extra Cash

In today's dynamic economy, finding new ways to generate extra income is more crucial than ever. While pursuing financial independence, side hustles present a formidable option to diversify your income streams, offering flexibility alongside your main career. They are not just a means to bolster your bank account—they're an opportunity to explore your passions, enhance your skills, and sometimes even pivot to a more rewarding full-time vocation.

Many people often underestimate the potential of a good side hustle. A side job can become a catalyst for honing entrepreneurial instincts and discovering hidden talents. Just ask anyone who's transformed a side project into a thriving business. With creativity and persistence, these ventures can eventually offer a blend of financial security and personal joy. They allow you to test the waters of entrepreneurship without the heavy risk of quitting your day job straight away.

The beauty of side hustles lies in their diversity. There's something for everyone, regardless of your skills or interests. Are you a crafty individual? Platforms like Etsy offer the perfect marketplace for handmade goods. Is writing your forte? Freelancing platforms such as Upwork or Fiverr provide ample opportunities to monetize your writing prowess. The digital world has virtually eliminated barriers to entry, making it easier than ever to reach potential customers worldwide.

Consider this practical approach: start by listing your skills and passions. Are there activities that you enjoy doing in your spare time or talents that others have complimented you on? These can be valuable clues to potential side hustles. From photography and designing to teaching online classes, the internet is teeming with possibilities to capitalize on what you love. Not only does this approach keep you motivated, but it can also lead to the elusive balance of meaningful and profitable work.

Freelancing is a popular side hustle choice that uses skillsets from your primary career. It's not constrained to just writing or graphic design; fields like software development, marketing, and consulting have a burgeoning demand for freelancers. By setting up a profile on freelance platforms and displaying your portfolio, you're able to reach a broad clientele. Although the competition can be stiff, consistency in delivering quality work will help build a robust reputation over time.

For those with a knack for sales, dipping a toe into *e-commerce* might be the perfect venture. Websites like eBay, Amazon, and Shopify allow you not only to sell goods but to track metrics and understand consumer behavior, laying a groundwork for potentially more significant future endeavors. Adopting a small-scale e-commerce business as a side hustle also helps grasp broader business strategies without overwhelming responsibilities.

Meanwhile, the digital age offers unconventional paths like creating content on platforms such as YouTube or TikTok. While initially, the road might seem saturated, focusing on niche topics or unique presentation styles can help carve out your special spot in this vast arena. As your audience grows, opportunities in ad revenue, sponsorships, and even merchandise emerge. Noticeable online personalities often start as passion projects, gravitating people with charismatic content delivery.

There's also immense promise in real estate as a side hustle. While it may require more initial capital and diligence than digital side projects, the returns can be significantly rewarding. You could explore renting out a spare room on Airbnb or refurbishing properties for a profit. Real estate inherently demands patience and meticulous research, which are invaluable skills in any business venture.

Time management stands out as a crucial skill for balancing side hustles with regular employment. To avoid burnout, carve out specific times during the week for your side venture activities, ensuring they don't encroach on your personal life. Seeing side hustles as separate from your main job is fundamental to maintaining equilibrium, ensuring that one doesn't derail the momentum of the other.

You must also embrace the learning curve associated with new hustles. Expect to make mistakes, and consider them as pivotal learning experiences instead of setbacks. These challenges are vital for personal and professional growth. Becoming resilient towards challenges and eager for new lessons will not only improve your side hustle but enrich your life journey.

Additionally, remember that every successful side hustle requires a **strategic plan** just like any business endeavor. You should outline your goals, understand your market, and analyze potential revenue streams. Establish short-term and long-term objectives, and keep track of your progress regularly. This framework provides a roadmap to measure success and make necessary adjustments along the way.

Ultimately, side hustles should align with your broader financial goals and lifestyle aspirations. Choose paths that not only infuse a healthy boost to your income but also contribute to your personal growth and happiness. By making intentional choices and following through with dedication, you're constructing a robust financial foundation and exploring roles that may hold the key to your ultimate professional fulfillment.

In conclusion, integrating side hustles into your multiple income streams isn't just about the extra cash. It's about reclaiming control over your financial destiny and creating doors to exciting new opportunities. Embrace the journey of experimentation and self-discovery that comes along with side hustles. They are an empowering step towards achieving long-lasting wealth and financial independence while living a life abundant in possibilities.

Chapter 10:
Leveraging Technology for Financial Success

In today's fast-paced world, technology isn't just a tool—it's a gateway to achieving financial success like never before. When you embrace digital innovations, you unlock countless opportunities to streamline your financial life. From cutting-edge budgeting apps that help you track and manage expenses effortlessly to dynamic online investment platforms that bring the world of stocks and bonds right to your fingertips, technology is leveling the playing field for everyone. It's time to seize these advantages and use them as a catalyst for your financial journey. By integrating smart technology into your wealth-building strategy, you're not just keeping pace with the digital age; you're paving your path to financial independence. Harness the power of technology, and watch your wealth-building potential thrive in ways that were once unimaginable. Whether you're setting your financial goals or want to maximize your returns, the right digital tools can empower you to make informed decisions quickly, confidently, and effectively.

Digital Tools for Budgeting

In the journey toward financial independence, one of your most powerful allies is technology. It simplifies the complex and amplifies the basics, empowering you to navigate your financial landscape with confidence and precision. Whether you're just starting to track your spending or you're managing a detailed, multi-tier financial plan, digital tools can transform how you budget and optimize your resources.

Budgeting isn't just about restricting spending. It's about creating a plan that supports your goals and dreams. With today's technology, tools like mobile apps and software programs make it easier than ever to control your finances. They offer a blend of convenience and accuracy that's hard to replicate manually. For instance, budgeting apps can automate tracking expenses, alert you to overspending, and provide real-time access to your financial summary. These tools offer unparalleled visibility into your financial habits, making it easier to identify areas where you can save.

Take advantage of automation. By using digital tools, you can automate your bill payments, savings transfers, and even investment contributions. Automation eliminates the stress of remembering deadlines and reduces the risk of incurring late fees. When your financial transactions happen without manual intervention, you're less likely to deviate from your budget, allowing your long-term strategies to unfold uninterrupted.

Digital budgeting tools also assist in setting and achieving financial goals. Many platforms allow you to set specific objectives, such as saving for a vacation, buying a home, or paying off debt. With these goals in place, tools can analyze your current spending patterns and suggest realistic plans to achieve them. The visual representation of progress in graphs and charts makes the often-intangible journey of wealth-building tangible and motivating.

Security is another critical benefit of digital tools. These applications come equipped with robust encryption and other security measures to safeguard your data. Of course, it's crucial to choose reputable applications to ensure your financial information is protected. It's worth researching and selecting tools with strong user reviews and high security ratings.

One of the overlooked advantages of digital budgeting is the ability to access and manage your finances from anywhere. Cloud-based tools mean your budget isn't tied to a singular device. Instead, whether you're on vacation, at work, or at home, your financial data travels with you. This accessibility ensures that you always have a real-time understanding of your financial health and can make informed decisions when opportunities or challenges arise.

Another powerful benefit of digital tools is their ability to integrate with other financial platforms. Many budgeting apps sync seamlessly with your bank accounts, credit cards, and investment portfolios, aggregating all financial data into one coherent dashboard. This holistic view allows for more strategic decision-making, helping you align your daily spending with your broader financial goals.

The customization these tools offer is another boon. As no two financial situations are identical, digital tools often allow for personalization. You can categorize expenses according to your lifestyle, set varying budget limits, and receive personalized tips based on your habits. Tailoring your budgeting tool to fit your unique financial situation ensures it works effectively for you, offering insights and control over areas you prioritize.

For those who feel overwhelmed by numbers, digital budgeting tools often simplify complex data. They translate raw figures into trends and patterns that are easy to understand. For instance, instead of being confronted with endless rows of spending data, you might see how much of your income goes to entertainment each month, making abstract concepts concrete and actionable.

Digital tools for budgeting also shine in their ability to teach and encourage good financial habits. Many platforms provide educational resources, tips for saving, and guidance on efficient financial management. This educational support can help users feel more in control and less stressed about their finances.

Embracing digital tools for budgeting not only makes managing finances more convenient but also embarks you on a path of continuous financial improvement. As you engage with these tools, you learn more about your financial behaviors and develop new habits that promote financial well-being. This knowledge and practice lay a strong foundation for building lasting wealth.

In conclusion, while achieving financial independence and creating wealth isn't solely about budgeting, it's a critical component of the broader strategy. Digital tools facilitate this process by making budgeting accessible, efficient, and integrated into your lifestyle. By leveraging these technologies, you're positioning yourself advantageously to track what you've earned, manage what you have, and plan for where you want to go. Using digital budgeting tools, you empower yourself to navigate the complexities of modern finances with ease and precision, setting the stage for a prosperous financial future.

Online Investment Platforms

In the rapidly evolving landscape of financial technology, online investment platforms have emerged as indispensable tools for individuals striving for financial independence and wealth accumulation. These platforms not only offer convenient access to various investment opportunities but also empower users with resources and insights that were once reserved for financial institutions and wealth managers. With the click of a button, you can now engage in stock trading, delve into real estate, or explore emerging markets from the comfort of your home. This democratization of finance is a game-changer, allowing anyone with an internet connection to take control of their financial destiny.

Let's not be mistaken, however. With great accessibility comes great responsibility. The platforms are a double-edged sword: they offer tremendous opportunities for growth but also require a savvy understanding of risks and strategic planning. It's essential to navigate these platforms with a clear set of financial goals and an awareness of your risk tolerance.

One of the significant advantages of online investment platforms is their low-cost structure compared to traditional brokerage firms. Users can enjoy reduced fees, which can significantly affect net returns over time. Moreover, such platforms often provide fractional shares, allowing investors with even modest funds to partake in the stock market. This inclusivity means that money once perceived as stagnant can now be put to work, potentially generating wealth that compounds over time.

Another profound benefit is the plethora of educational resources these platforms offer. Many provide real-time data, analytics, and insights that can help users make informed decisions. These features often include news feeds, stock research tools, and webinars, all of which serve to educate and empower investors, transforming them from mere passive participants to knowledgeable stakeholders in their own financial journey.

Yet, the heartening success stories often shared by these platforms shouldn't distract from the necessity of developing a disciplined approach to investing. It's easy to get caught up in market trends or social media hype, but true financial success lies in a consistent strategy aligned with your long-term goals. This discipline can be cultivated through setting clear, measurable objectives and maintaining a diversified portfolio that aligns with your personal risk profile.

Online investment platforms also offer automated services, such as robo-advisors, which provide algorithm-driven financial planning services with little to no human supervision. These robo-advisors can tailor investment advice to individual needs, taking into account factors such as age, life goals, and risk tolerance. Made popular for their convenience and efficiency, they afford an excellent solution for those who may lack the time or expertise to manage their investments actively. With these digital marvels at our disposal, you can potentially maximize your returns without the need for an expensive traditional financial advisor.

However, amidst all the innovations and conveniences, users must remain aware of cybersecurity risks. The increase in digital transactions has also elevated the risk of data breaches and fraudulent activities. It's crucial to utilize platforms with robust security measures in place and to practice personal digital safety habits, such as using strong, unique passwords and enabling two-factor authentication.

Another aspect to consider is the aspect of emotional investing, which can be exacerbated by the speed and accessibility of online platforms. Fast-paced environments may tempt investors into making impulsive decisions driven by fear or greed—often a recipe for financial disaster. Achieving financial success requires recognizing these emotions and adhering to a strategic plan, even when market turbulence arises.

It's also worth mentioning that platforms vary widely in the types of investments they offer beyond traditional stocks and bonds. Some provide access to alternative investment opportunities such as cryptocurrencies, peer-to-peer lending, or real estate investment trusts (REITs). These alternatives can add a layer of diversification to a portfolio, but they come with their risks and complexities. Anyone considering such ventures should research thoroughly and potentially consult with a professional.

As we observe, the future of investing is undoubtedly digital, and online platforms will continue to evolve, offering even more advanced tools and opportunities. Staying informed about new features and emerging platforms can position you well in this ever-changing landscape. Keep in mind, the key to leveraging these resources successfully is continuous learning and adaptation. Embrace the technology at your fingertips, but never forgo the timeless principles of prudent investing—knowledge, patience, and discipline.

As we chart our journey toward financial independence, leveraging online investment platforms effectively can be one of the most powerful tools at our disposal. It's not just about making money; it's about making informed, wise decisions that align with our values and long-term objectives. The potential for growth and prosperity is immense for those who harness the power of these platforms wisely, ensuring that their money isn't merely spent, but invested in a future filled with possibility.

Chapter 11:
Navigating Tax Strategies

In the quest for financial independence, understanding and utilizing effective tax strategies can significantly accelerate your wealth-building journey. Taxes aren't just a yearly obligation; they're a constant element of your financial landscape that, when maneuvered wisely, can be transformed into an advantage. By exploring tax-efficient investing, you'll find ways to minimize the impact of taxes on your portfolio returns, thus enhancing your capital growth. As an entrepreneur, strategic tax planning is crucial—not only for preserving hard-earned income but for reinvesting in your business's expansion. Every dollar saved is a dollar that can fuel future opportunities, building a more robust financial future. Mastering the art of tax navigation isn't just about compliance; it's about creating leverage in your financial strategy. Equip yourself with the knowledge to make informed decisions, keeping more of your wealth in your hands and working to secure your long-term financial success.

Tax Efficient Investing

When it comes to building wealth, taxes often feel like an unwelcome companion. Yet, understanding tax efficient investing can turn this gameplay to your favor, enhancing your journey to financial independence. To put it simply, tax efficiency is about structuring your investment portfolio in ways that minimize your tax liabilities.

The key is knowing which investments to hold in tax-advantaged accounts and which are better suited for taxable accounts.

Imagine optimizing your portfolio in a way that maximizes your returns, not just before taxes but after taxes too. Your future self would definitely thank you for this foresight, as investing isn't just about picking the right stocks or funds; it's about choosing the right accounts to hold them in. Essentially, tax efficient investing is like crafting a strategy with multiple layers, where each decision is meticulously made to preserve and grow your wealth.

First, let's talk about asset location. This concept refers to the strategic placement of different types of investments in either taxable or tax-advantaged accounts, like IRAs or 401(k)s. Typically, it's beneficial to hold income-generating assets that have higher tax burdens—such as bonds—in tax-deferred accounts. This is because the tax deferral allows the interest they earn to grow without the yearly tax drag, delaying tax payments until you're likely in a lower tax bracket during retirement.

On the flip side, consider placing investments that benefit from lower capital gains taxes, like stocks, in taxable accounts. This strategy allows you to potentially take advantage of lower long-term capital gains rates and the ability to manage tax impacts through techniques like tax-loss harvesting. By doing this, you're paying attention to the current tax laws and positioning your investments in a way that maintains more of your money in your pocket.

Tax-loss harvesting, a technique mentioned above, is one of the most effective and commonly used strategies in tax efficient investing. In practice, it means selling securities at a loss to offset capital gains of similar or different securities, ultimately reducing your overall tax bill. The principle is simple: if an investment in your portfolio declines, you can sell it to realize a loss that counters gains you've already made. Moreover, any excess loss can often be used to offset up to $3,000 of ordinary income each year, with remaining losses carried over to future years.

While tax-loss harvesting can lower your tax liabilities, another strategic player is the Roth IRA. Contributions to a Roth IRA are made with after-tax dollars, which means your money grows tax-free, and you don't have to pay taxes when you withdraw it in retirement. This kind of account is especially valued for its tax-free withdrawals, providing a significant advantage if you expect to be in a higher tax bracket later in life. Furthermore, there are no required minimum distributions, allowing your investments within a Roth IRA to continue compounding tax-free for as long as you please.

Beyond investment accounts, there's also the tax efficiency of diversified investments like ETFs and index funds. These are traditionally more tax efficient than mutual funds due to their unique structure and trading mechanism. ETFs, for example, generally incur fewer capital gains distributions than mutual funds due to how they're traded and managed. This means you have more control over when you realize those gains, which plays neatly into managing your taxable income and tax strategy.

Investment strategies using municipal bonds can also contribute to tax efficient investing. Municipal bonds, issued by local governments, offer interest payments that are exempt from federal taxes—and sometimes state and local taxes if you're a resident of the issuing state. They typically offer lower yields than taxable bonds, but the tax savings can make a significant difference for investors in higher tax brackets, offering a tax-equivalent yield that's competitive.

While executing a tax-efficient strategy can sound complex, it's about understanding the principles and tailoring them to your financial situation. It's vital to regularly revisit and revise your strategy as tax laws change, and as you proceed along your wealth-building journey. Partnering with a knowledgeable tax advisor or financial planner might also be beneficial to ensure you're leveraging the best tax-saving strategies available to you.

Ultimately, being strategic about taxes can significantly influence your path to financial freedom. A strong grasp of tax-efficient investing empowers you to keep more of your hard-earned money, potentially accelerating your journey to achieving life goals. By honing this section of your financial toolkit, you're not just investing in the market; you're investing in your future—a future where your wealth is not just created but efficiently preserved. Remember, in the grand scheme of wealth-building, every dollar saved is indeed a dollar earned.

Tax Planning for Entrepreneurs

In the ever-evolving landscape of entrepreneurship, the distinction between success and failure often hinges on the ability to manage finances wisely. Effective tax planning is not just a nice-to-have, but a critical pillar of your business strategy. As an entrepreneur, planning your taxes is like laying a strong foundation for your enterprise. Skipping this crucial step is akin to building your house on sand. While taxes can seem burdensome, with the right strategies, they become tools of empowerment and growth.

One of the most compelling reasons for entrepreneurs to engage in thoughtful tax planning is the direct impact it can have on cash flow. Cash is the lifeblood of any business, and by understanding various tax deductions, credits, and incentives available, you can significantly enhance your cash reserves. Imagine being able to reinvest saved funds into your business for expansion, hiring new talent, or upgrading technology. Tax planning facilitates these opportunities by keeping more capital within reach.

Consider, for example, the importance of structuring your business entity appropriately. The decision between operating as a sole proprietor, a partnership, a limited liability company (LLC), or an S corporation is not merely a legal formality. Each structure comes with its unique set of tax implications, affecting how profits are taxed and what deductions can be claimed. For instance, an LLC typically offers flexibility in how you're taxed, which can be optimized further by being taxed as an S corporation. This decision can mean the difference between tax-efficient growth and losing valuable funds to liabilities that could be mitigated.

Deductions are another essential area where entrepreneurs can realize substantial savings. Business expenses such as office supplies, rent, utilities, and even certain travel expenses can be deducted, reducing your taxable income. Additionally, home office deductions are particularly valuable in the current era of remote work. By understanding what constitutes a legitimate business expense and keeping meticulous records, you dramatically improve your bottom line. However, knowing precisely what qualifies for a deduction requires careful attention to IRS guidelines, ensuring compliance and avoiding pitfalls like audits.

Entrepreneurs should also be keenly aware of the benefits that retirement plans provide. Establishing a retirement savings plan for yourself and your employees not only secures your future but also offers immediate tax advantages. Contributions to retirement plans are often tax-deductible, and various plan options, such as SEP IRAs and Solo 401(k)s, cater specifically to business owners and self-employed individuals. This not only reduces current taxable income but ensures that you're planning wisely for the future—a crucial dual benefit for those forging their own paths.

But there's more to tax planning than deductions and credits. Timing plays a pivotal role too. For instance, deferring income to the next tax year or accelerating expenses into the current year can substantially shift tax burdens. Knowing when to execute these strategies can leverage tax laws to your advantage. Such maneuvers require foresight and an understanding of both current and projected financial landscapes.

Furthermore, staying informed about changes in tax legislation is indispensable. Tax laws are subject to frequent revisions, influenced by political shifts and economic policies. An entrepreneur must stay informed to remain agile and proactive. This might mean consulting with a tax professional regularly—not just during tax season—to stay ahead of changes and insights that can affect your planning.

Tax incentives for research and development (R&D) present another avenue for growth-oriented entrepreneurs. If innovation is at the heart of your business, the R&D tax credit can be a powerful ally. By actively pursuing innovation and improvement within your products or services, you qualify for these credits, directly reducing your tax bill. This, in turn, empowers businesses to allocate funds toward further innovation, feeding a cycle of growth and development.

Understanding international tax considerations is crucial for entrepreneurs aspiring to expand beyond domestic borders. International tax laws offer both challenges and opportunities. Multinational operations have to grapple with complex issues like transfer pricing, foreign tax credits, and variable corporate tax rates. While these can be daunting, they also provide opportunities for beneficial tax strategies that can improve a company's global financial efficiency. Knowledgeable tax planning in this arena is indispensable to avoid pitfalls that come with managing cross-border transactions.

While the intricacies of tax regulation might seem daunting, the right mindset is instrumental. Approaching tax planning with a proactive, positive perspective transforms what many assume is a burden into a strategic asset. This shift in perspective requires moving beyond mere compliance with tax laws toward a more comprehensive strategy for wealth-building and business enhancement.

Lastly, technology is an indispensable tool in the entrepreneur's tax strategy toolkit. Digital accounting and tax software streamline the collection and organization of data, allowing for more accurate filings and timely insights. They offer functionalities that simplify record-keeping, track expenses in real time, and highlight potential deductions. Such tools serve not only to improve efficiency but also to prepare entrepreneurs for increasingly digital tax audits and interfaces, ensuring preparedness for the future of tax compliance.

In conclusion, tax planning is more than a necessary task—it's an empowering strategy that paves the way for entrepreneurial success. By understanding the nuances of tax law and leveraging available tools and incentives, entrepreneurs can significantly enhance their financial health and resilience. Remember, mastery over taxes is akin to unlocking a new level of potential within your enterprise. With the right strategies and mindset, taxes become less of a burden and more of a catalyst for achieving your financial independence and creating lasting wealth.

Chapter 12:
Philanthropy and Legacy Planning

As you move beyond the foundational stages of wealth-building, your focus naturally shifts to the impact and legacy you wish to leave behind. This is where philanthropy and legacy planning come into play, integrating the heart and mind of financial independence. Thoughtful giving is not just about donating money; it's an opportunity to influence and inspire change in ways only you can. Establish your legacy by aligning your philanthropic efforts with your core values, ensuring they resonate with your life's purpose and pass down your vision to future generations. Whether you're setting up a charitable foundation, creating a trust, or planning your estate, it's vital to mesh emotional satisfaction with financial strategy. Your legacy reflects not just your financial acumen but also the intention to create a better world for those who follow, showcasing that true wealth transcends beyond personal gain to meaningful generosity.

Giving Back to the Community

In the journey toward financial independence, it's easy to become completely focused on personal wealth-building. However, a truly fulfilling life isn't measured solely by assets and financial statements. It's about the legacy you leave behind and the impact you make. Giving back to the community isn't just a moral obligation; it can enrich your own life substantially, creating a genuine sense of purpose and fulfillment.

Imagine the ripple effects your generosity can spawn. By using resources effectively to foster community growth or support crucial causes, you inspire others to do the same. You don't need to be a billionaire to make a difference; even modest contributions can ignite significant change. In the grand tapestry of financial independence, philanthropy serves as more than just a cornerstone—it's a catalyst for enduring impact.

Moreover, giving transcends monetary donations. Your time and skills are just as valuable. Volunteering for local organizations or offering mentorship can have profound effects, both for the community and yourself. By sharing the wisdom of your own journey toward financial independence, you empower others to pursue theirs. This cycle of empowerment fosters collective growth and a stronger, more resilient society.

One of the most effective ways to give back is through strategic philanthropy. This approach involves carefully selecting causes that align with your values and long-term goals. Strategic philanthropy allows you to maximize your impact while ensuring your contributions are meaningful. It requires evaluating where your resources can have the largest impact and being deliberate about how you allocate your money, time, and expertise.

Of course, giving shouldn't be an afterthought. It should be an integral part of your financial planning, woven seamlessly into the fabric of your wealth-building strategy. A thoughtfully crafted charitable plan not only reflects your values but can also offer significant tax benefits. Tax efficiencies in charitable donations can strengthen your ability to continue supporting the causes you care about, making your philanthropy more sustainable and impactful.

Consider establishing a donor-advised fund as a means of organizing your charitable efforts. These funds offer flexibility, allowing you to donate appreciated assets like stocks or bonds, which can be more beneficial than cash donations. Plus, they provide immediate tax benefits while giving you time to decide which causes to fund. This setup grants you the opportunity to be both spontaneous and strategic with your giving.

Estate planning is another vital component of legacy building and can be a powerful vehicle for philanthropy. By including charitable bequests in your will, your legacy of giving will endure beyond your lifetime. You might also consider trusts that can benefit your family while ensuring lasting support for your chosen charities. Not only does this create a legacy of generosity, but it can also offer peace of mind knowing your values will continue to echo through future generations.

In recent years, philanthropic efforts have evolved thanks to technology and social media, which have opened new avenues and expanded traditional boundaries of giving. Crowdfunding platforms like GoFundMe or Kickstarter enable you to directly support small, grassroots initiatives. These platforms break down geographical constraints and connect you to causes in need, broadening your ability to create impact on both a local and global scale.

Now, let's not overlook small-scale acts of kindness and personal impact. Small gestures, such as supporting local businesses, sponsoring school events, or donating supplies to shelters, accumulate over time and create substantial benefits. Communities thrive on mutual support and collective goodwill. By embracing a giving mindset, your contributions become a crucial part of a thriving ecosystem of support.

Part of giving back is creating a culture of philanthropy within your circles. Inspire your family and friends to engage in giving. Share your motivations, experiences, and the emotional and social returns you've gained. Building a network of likeminded givers can amplify impact significantly. Together, you're able to form dedicated, organized groups that can tackle bigger projects or causes than any one individual might be able to do alone.

Legacy planning through philanthropy isn't strictly about financial contributions or big gestures. It's about the intention behind the act of giving. When you prioritize community enrichment, you're not just investing in others; you're investing in yourself, your character, and ultimately, your happiness. Wealth is an incredible tool that can change lives. Through grassroots efforts, innovative strategies, and selfless giving, wealth becomes not just a measure of personal success but a conduit for widespread good.

Integrating philanthropy into your wealth-building journey empowers you to become a beacon of hope for others, reinforcing a cycle of prosperity and benevolence. As you navigate your path to financial independence, remember the profound influence you can wield through thoughtful acts of charity. By giving back, you not only reinforce the foundation of your own legacy but you also build a better future for everyone.

Estate Planning Basics

When it comes to achieving financial independence, understanding estate planning basics is crucial for safeguarding the wealth you build. Estate planning isn't just about distributing your assets when you pass; it's about creating a strategic blueprint that ensures your financial legacy aligns with your values and desires. Getting ahead with estate planning empowers you to make a tangible impact long after you're gone, allowing your wealth to contribute to causes, businesses, and people you care about most. Let's dive into what estate planning entails and why it's essential for sculpting a lasting legacy.

Estate planning begins with a simple but powerful concept: preparedness. By drafting a will, you set the foundation for how your estate will be handled, thus providing clarity and reducing potential disputes among your beneficiaries. The will is where you express your personal wishes regarding the division of your properties and assets.

Without it, your estate could be subjected to the whims of state laws, which rarely align perfectly with individual intentions. Drafting a will isn't an act of pessimism; it's a step toward ensuring your hard-earned wealth is utilized in ways you find meaningful.

Beyond the will, consider establishing a trust. Trusts are versatile tools that offer privacy, tax benefits, and more control over your assets. They can bypass the sometimes lengthy and expensive probate process and specify exactly how and when your beneficiaries receive their inheritance. This can be particularly beneficial if you have young children, special-needs relatives, or beneficiaries who might not be ready to handle a large sum of money responsibly. Trusts can vary from revocable to irrevocable, each serving different purposes and providing unique advantages in your estate arsenal.

As you embark on your estate planning journey, remember that the heart of the process is your own unique goals and values. Ask yourself: What legacy do I want to leave behind? Whether it's supporting charity, sustaining a family business, or safeguarding your children's education, articulate these objectives clearly. Work with a financial advisor or estate planner to tailor a plan that meshes with these aspirations. Keep in mind, estate planning isn't a one-time event. It's a dynamic blueprint that should evolve as life circumstances change, whether through marriage, the birth of a child, or financial growth.

Moreover, don't overlook the importance of healthcare directives and powers of attorney. These documents ensure that your financial and health-related decisions are in trusted hands if you're ever incapacitated. This layer of planning isn't just about making economic arrangements; it offers peace of mind to your family, knowing they're carrying out your wishes during difficult times. Living wills, for example, specifically outline your preferences regarding medical treatments, thus preventing potential conflicts and alleviating emotional burdens on loved ones.

While planning your estate, one can't underscore enough the significance of tax considerations. Understanding and leveraging tax laws can prevent your estate from being unnecessarily depleted. Estate taxes, gift taxes, and capital gains taxes can take a substantial chunk out of your estate if not properly managed. There are numerous strategies to mitigate these taxes, from lifetime giving to charitable donations, which not only optimize your estate's value but also extend your philanthropic impact. An informed estate plan seeks to balance asset preservation with potential tax liabilities.

Communication plays a vital role in estate planning. Conversations with your beneficiaries and loved ones can prevent misunderstandings and set clear expectations about your estate's disposition. Within these dialogues, you can impart the values and intentions driving your decisions, making your legacy not just a matter of wealth but a personal narrative. Being transparent creates an opportunity for your family to understand not just what they'll receive, but the meaning behind your decisions. This transforms your estate from a collection of assets to a testament of your life's work.

For those deeply engaged in creating a lasting legacy, consider charitable vehicles like donor-advised funds (DAFs) or private foundations. With DAFs, you retain advisory privileges on fund distribution during your lifetime, providing a strategic and flexible approach to philanthropy. Establishing a private foundation, while more complex, gives you unparalleled control over your charitable endeavors, often allowing for perpetual good, managed according to guiding principles you establish. Whether large or small, these vehicles magnify your impact on the world in ways few other methods can.

Estate planning may raise uncomfortable questions and involve confronting our own mortality. However, with focus and foresight, it becomes a powerful exercise in self-determination. It provides an opportunity to secure the financial future for your loved ones in alignment with your values while also setting an example of thoughtful financial stewardship. Recurring reviews and updates to your estate plan ensure it remains relevant, resonant, and robust amidst life's inevitable changes.

As you weave through the complexities and considerations, an estate plan emerges as the final stitch in the tapestry of financial independence. It combines foresight, strategic thinking, and emotional intelligence to curate not just a path for your wealth, but a continued testament to your life's vision and dedication. Now is the time to reflect on what you want your wealth to achieve, setting the stage for a legacy that celebrates not just financial success but the essence of who you are.

Conclusion

As we reach the end of this journey toward financial independence and wealth-building, it's vital to take a moment to reflect on the path we've traveled. Financial freedom isn't just about accumulating wealth; it's the empowerment you gain from understanding and controlling your financial future. This book has been your guide to breaking down complex concepts into actionable steps, providing you with the foundation to not only aim for prosperity but to achieve it.

Think about the transformation you've embarked upon from the very first page to this conclusion. You've learned how to master personal finance starting with the basics of budgeting and debt management. These are not merely chores to complete but are fundamental building blocks in securing your peace of mind. Establishing a strong personal finance framework lays the groundwork for everything that follows, providing stability and direction.

As you delved into saving strategies, the importance of an emergency fund and retirement accounts unfolded. They've offered you not just a sense of security but also a glimpse into what a strategically planned future looks like. By setting aside funds for emergencies and retirement, you're not merely saving money—you're buying peace of mind and freedom for your future self.

The chapters on investment foundations and advanced techniques have opened up new worlds of opportunity. Understanding stocks, bonds, mutual funds, and more complex investment vehicles empowers you to grow your wealth actively. Whether you've chosen to explore real estate, venture into alternative investments, or both, the knowledge you've gained enables you to make informed decisions that align with your financial goals.

Entrepreneurship stands out as a powerful pathway to financial success. Starting and scaling a business can be daunting yet immensely rewarding. With the strategies discussed, you now appreciate that entrepreneurship isn't merely about innovation but also about persistence, adaptability, and learning to leverage the tools at your disposal to drive growth and success.

Cultivating a wealth mindset has perhaps been one of your most significant shifts. By identifying and overcoming psychological barriers, you've embraced the power of financial goals to shape your future. Developing this mindset isn't just about fostering positivity but adopting a proactive approach to life, setting ambitious yet realistic goals, and persistently pursuing them until they're achieved.

Risk management emerged as an essential part of your wealth-building toolkit. Protecting assets through insurance and various safety nets ensures that your hard-earned gains are safeguarded against unforeseen circumstances. You've learned not just the technicalities of risk management but the peace of mind it offers when navigating your financial journey.

The exploration of multiple income streams, whether through passive income or side hustles, has been key to diversifying your revenue and building financial resilience. These ventures not only augment your primary income source but also provide avenues for personal and professional growth.

Technology is reshaping the financial landscape, offering remarkable tools and platforms for managing finances, budgeting, and investing. By leveraging cutting-edge tech solutions, you've allowed yourself to work smarter, not harder, and keep pace with an ever-evolving world.

Tax strategies, though often overlooked or misunderstood, have been demystified for you, providing tangible ways to retain and grow your wealth. Understanding how to efficiently navigate tax systems can ultimately leave more capital in your hands, capital that can be reinvested in ventures that further your wealth-building strategy.

Philanthropy and legacy planning bind your journey by focusing on giving back and crafting a future legacy. The true measure of wealth is not the amount you accumulate but the impact you make with it. By planning thoughtfully for your legacy, you're ensuring that your wealth serves both your family's future and the community at large.

To conclude, the principles and strategies outlined in this book are more than just tactics—they form a comprehensive philosophy of financial empowerment. You now possess the tools and insights needed to forge your own path to lasting wealth. Keep these lessons close, continue to learn and adapt, and remember that financial independence isn't a destination but a dynamic journey. You're equipped to navigate the financial world with confidence and create the prosperous future you've always envisioned.

Further
Resources and Readings

Achieving financial independence and building lasting wealth is a journey filled with both challenges and opportunities. As you continue to enhance your understanding and skills, it's important to have access to the right resources and further readings. This section is designed to guide you towards materials and tools that can provide deeper insights and enhance your wealth-building strategies.

Books to Expand Your Financial Literacy

- **"The Millionaire Next Door"** by Thomas J. Stanley and William D. Danko – Gain insights into the spending and saving habits of America's wealth-building citizens.

- **"The Intelligent Investor"** by Benjamin Graham – Discover foundational principles for smart investing and understanding market fluctuations.

- **"Your Money or Your Life"** by Vicki Robin and Joe Dominguez – Explore the relationship between your values and your finances with practical steps to achieve financial independence.

Online Platforms and Courses

- **Coursera and Udacity** – Explore courses in personal finance and investment strategies tailored for beginners to advanced learners.

- **Investopedia** – Engage in a wealth of articles and tutorials covering all aspects of investing, saving, and personal finance.

- **Khan Academy** – Offers free courses on finance and capital markets, providing foundational knowledge for better wealth management.

Podcasts and Blogs

- **"The Dave Ramsey Show"** – Practical advice for managing money and achieving financial peace.

- **"ChooseFI"** – Discussions that highlight strategies for financial independence and early retirement.

- **"Mr. Money Mustache's Blog"** – A fun approach to frugality, with tips on retiring early and living financially independently.

Tools and Apps for Financial Management

- **Mint and YNAB (You Need A Budget)** – Budgeting apps that help track spending, create budgets, and ensure financial goals are met.

- **Personal Capital** – A comprehensive tool for managing investments and offering a holistic view of your financial health.

- **Acorns and Robinhood** – Platforms providing easy access for beginners to start investing with minimal amounts and learn about stock trading.

In your pursuit of financial independence, education is a powerful ally. By continually expanding your knowledge base, you'll not only enhance your skills but also boost your confidence in making informed financial decisions. Let these resources inspire and guide you as you work towards financial prosperity and independence.

www.ingramcontent.com/pod-product-compliance
Lightning Source LLC
Chambersburg PA
CBHW022116170526
45157CB00004B/1672